PROJECT MANAGEMENT
FOR WRITERS:

Get Focused, Get Organized, Get It Done!

PROJECT MANAGEMENT
FOR WRITERS:

Get Focused, Get Organized, Get It Done!

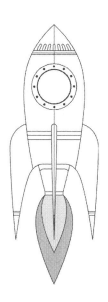

TERRY STAFFORD

Published by Tipperary South Publishing
4216 S. Mooney Blvd., Suite #317
Visalia, CA 93277-9143

ISBN: 978-0-9859655-9-4 (trade paperback)
ISBN: 978-0-9859655-8-7 (eBook)

Library of Congress Control Number: 2020921023

Cover and Interior Design by JD&J Book Cover Design, LLC
Editing by Harshman Services

To all of the writers of the world:
Your message is important.
It can change lives.
Don't keep it hidden.

SPECIAL INVITATION

Many like-minded individuals have gathered in an online community to share ideas, render support, and promote accountability. When the idea for Project Management for Writers first came to me, I knew it was time to create this gathering place where we can all help each other become better writers and project managers.

I'd like to personally invite you to join the Project Management for Writers Mastermind at Facebook.com/groups/projectmanagementforwriters where you will find motivation, daily support, and help with any of your writing questions.

You can connect with me personally on Facebook.com/AuthorTerryStafford or through my website at ItsaWriterfulLife.com, where you can also subscribe to my newsletter.

Thank you so much for investing your precious time and resources into this project. I look forward to connecting with you and hearing about your book soon!

Table Of Contents

INTRODUCTION

Project Management for Writers is not another diatribe on how to publish a book, though if you manage your projects correctly, one should assume a book can be published if that's your desired outcome.

Many articles have reported that most Americans want to write a book. Some say eighty-seven percent. A much smaller number of those Americans actually start a book. Few of them, perhaps three percent, actually follow through to the more painful steps of finishing and publishing it. I've not been able to find any documented studies to prove these statistics, but it's safe to say that many more people want to write a book than actually do it.

Think of all those times that you've said, "I should write a book." Or perhaps you've been told on many occasions, "You should write a book!" But you shove it off to the back of your mind as some impractical pipe dream. "Maybe someday."

All too often, once you decide that you should write a book, you freeze. "How? What do I do?" You immediately jump into perfectionist mode and proclaim that you could never write like [enter name of famous author here], so why bother. Even when you manage to get something written, you might ask, "What do I do next?"

When I started writing books, it didn't take long to discover that it can be a repeatable process. Once established, you no longer have to think about the how. Don't let the term *repeatable process* put you off. You see, I spent most of my adult life as a project manager overseeing many development and process management projects for NASA, both at the Marshall Space Flight Center in Huntsville, Alabama, and Kennedy Space Center near Cape Canaveral, Florida.

During those thirty-plus years, I became a certified Project Management Professional, studying and taking a long arduous exam administered by the Project Management Institute (PMI). Great! Whatever that means. So, what does all that have to do with writing?

I'll say it again. Repeatable processes. Project management is all about repeatable processes. Once you've cleared a path to success, you don't have to keep clearing it. In other words, you don't have to keep reinventing the wheel. PMI provides a framework through which almost any project must be—or at least can be—managed. Of course, different industries have different requirements that result in different workflows and terminology. Nevertheless, when you look at them closely, you'll see that the basic framework is the same. How that relates to writing a book can be found in PMI's definition.

A project is a temporary endeavor undertaken to create
a unique product, service, or result.

That's it? Yep. Simple as that. A project is temporary in that it has a beginning and an end and results in the form of a deliverable. Do you see it? Your book is that deliverable—the product. How you define the end of the project is up to you. It could simply be when you write "The End" at the bottom of your manuscript. It could be when you get it back from your editor and file it away for some future date or purpose. Perhaps it's when you email the final pdf document to your friends and family. Or, hopefully, the end is that glorious day when you launch your published book for all the world to see.

As I wrote my second and third books, those repeatable processes gradually became more obvious; I could see how these projects fit the framework that PMI so eloquently provided. Each book was, indeed, a project to be passed through the same set of steps toward an ultimate goal. Unfortunately, authors all too often begin writing their second or third book without this in mind, trying to reinvent the wheel as though they had never done it before. They start creating tools and devices, forgetting that they created them when they wrote their previous book.

Photo by Wonderlane on Unsplash

Things are lying all over the place, both on their computer and on their desk, while their mind is distracted from the task at hand—writing the book. In the beginning, I often found myself wanting to clean my desk or reorganize my office when it came time to sit down and write. Trying to create new processes provides convenient distractions from the actual practice of writing. Repeatable processes help you avoid these dreadful author pitfalls.

You might find it interesting to note that a Program is an ongoing endeavor, i.e.—no discernible end, that can be made up of multiple Projects. If and when you start writing a series, for example, it may be helpful for the anal retentive among us to consider it a Program. So, a trilogy would be three Projects within a single Program.)

I've mentioned PMI's framework a few times now. So, what is it? Quite simply, it's the layout of this book. It's the Table of Contents, if you will. It's all the wickets you need to get through to end up with a professionally written masterpiece ready for publication or, if you wish, filing away. Your call. Here are the areas we will define and discuss throughout this book. These are called the 10 Project Management Knowledge Areas by PMI.

Integration Management

Scope Management

Time Management

Cost Management

Quality Management

Human Resources Management

Communications Management

Risk Management

Procurement Management

Stakeholder Management

Keep in mind that there is nothing necessarily sequential about this list overall. The specific task sequence will come in Time Management. These areas might even sound a bit daunting for the simple act of writing a book, but don't let it overwhelm you. This will simply give you a framework from which to manage your writing practice. Once you have your workflow identified, you won't have to think about it much anymore. Of course, you will likely want to fine-tune it with Lessons Learned from time to time, but workflow will be established. If you aren't familiar with what Lessons Learned are, it's exactly what it sounds like. We'll discuss it near the end of the book.

To be fair, NASA has entire organizations and infrastructure spread around the country to handle each one of these disciplines. It's your tax dollars at work. But when you consider that they sent people to the moon with computing power less than that of a Commodore 64 (remember those?), you won't need those masses of people to launch your book. It was done with the brainpower of the people in those organizations. The movie *Hidden Figures* comes to mind, if you'd like to see behind the scenes at NASA in those days.

While we won't get tangled up in the intricacies of this framework, we can use it to lead us through what we need in order to plan, write, and prepare to publish a book. Then, because you have the framework, you can do it over and over again without getting wrapped around the axle on processes, feeling like you've never done it before each time you open a new manuscript file.

Of course, you will come upon your own *how* once you understand the *what*. Only you will know your environment and what makes you feel creative. Maybe it's writing in a barn using a #2 pencil and a legal pad. It happens. Maybe it's writing on a high-end MacBook Pro computer using a specialized software application like Scrivener. Maybe it's somewhere in between.

Regardless of the *how*, the *what* remains. It is my goal here to walk you through this framework to help you define your own repeatable process that will lead you to your prolific writing success, whether you choose to publish or not.

Let's get started, shall we?

1.

INTEGRATION MANAGEMENT

What is Integration Management?

We'll start with PMI's definition.

Integration Management is a collection of processes required to ensure that the various elements of the projects are properly coordinated. It involves making tradeoffs among competing objectives and alternatives to meet or exceed stakeholder needs and expectations. Comprised of: Project plan development.

While it is a mouthful, it does apply to writing a book—just not in the same way it applied to launching a Space Shuttle to the International Space Station. So, what are stakeholders and expectations? It is, indeed, the crux of the above statement. Stakeholder Management has its own chapter in this book. But in a nutshell, stakeholders are the people that have an interest or are invested in your work—the ones who care. Your editor, your book cover designer, your interior designer, your publishers, the influencers you enlist to help spread the word; they all have an interest in your book. But wait! Let's not forget the most important stakeholders of all—your readers.

As the project manager—oh, that's you, by the way, the author—it is your job to understand the objectives or expectations of each of your stakeholders. And, believe it or not, they aren't the same. The only one who cares about the whole thing is you. Readers care about the story. Book cover designers care about the message they can create while designing around technical issues like spine width. Your interior designer doesn't care about the story. They care about matching a genre expectation for paper color and print style.

If you use Amazon KDP as your distributor, they don't give a rip about any of that. They are only interested in sales. Their profits are based on the number of books ordered and printed or downloaded. More is better, and that is their objective.

Putting all of those objectives together into a cohesive set of requirements is your job as the project manager . . . excuse me . . . author.

Things You'll Need to Do

So, with the Integration Management responsibility in mind, what are the things you need to decide? Allow me to list a few. But before I do, if you're just starting out as an author, *do not* allow this stuff to overwhelm you. If there is only one thing I could say that you should be doing, even if nothing else happens, it is this.

Write.
Your.
Book.

That's it! Above all else, just sit down and write. Stay focused and get it done. If that's all you can think of right now, that's fine. These other things are merely to help you get organized as you make your way through the process wickets.

So, what are those decisions? You've likely heard it before: Who? What? When? Where? Why? How?

- Who is the ideal reader for this book?
- What will you write about?
- When will you write?
- Where will you write?
- Why are you writing?
- How will you write?

Let's take these questions one at a time.

Who is the ideal reader for this book?

This might take a little work on your part. Actually, all of this is going to take work on your part, but I digress. You'll need to think about the person you are writing to. Are they needing to learn something? Do they simply want to be entertained? What kind of entertainment do they want? Are they needing a textbook or a how-to book? Fact based or conversational?

More often than not, this is about psychographics and not so much, demographics. While you can certainly identify age groups, gender, profession, financial status, etc., especially for genre-specific nonfiction works, you are usually better served by identifying the itch you are trying to scratch. How does your reader feel about life? What is their worldview? What is their pain point? Interestingly, these people are you. Because you know you. You generally write for you.

Writing for *you* means simply writing for people like you. So, start there. That's it.

Q: Who is my ideal reader?

A: People like me.

Boom! But be prepared to define what that means. Get a picture in your mind of the one person that personifies you but isn't you. Write to that person. Some content creators will even put a picture of that person up on their computer monitor so they never forget who they are writing (or speaking) to.

What will you write about?

Oh, yeah. That. Well, that's up to you. Are you going to teach your readers something, or are you going to share your experiences? Maybe you just want to create a world and tell a fun story to entertain your audience. The possibilities are endless. Brainstorming in a journal will help you capture ideas. It's often said that everyone has a heart book—the one that's been hiding inside them for years. Sometimes, you just need to get that book out of your system first so you can move on to other books. Even if it's not a commercial success, it's great practice, and it gets what's in your heart down on paper. It might be a personal story of pain or a time in your family's history that you want to make sure is never forgotten. My first novel, *Strings of Faith*, was a story to honor a special young girl in my family who tragically left us far too soon.

The fact that you're even wanting to get organized by learning about project management tells me that you already have ideas flying around. Maybe you've already written a book or even several, and you're wanting to polish your skills. Capture those ideas!

How often have you been driving down the road when you get an idea for a story or an anecdote for a lesson and are afraid you're going to forget it?

Wait. Forget what?

Yep. Just like that. Gone. Buh-bye.

Figure out a system for capturing those ideas. I use Evernote. But Apple Notes, One Note, and many other tools will work just fine if you live in a digital world. Having a journal with you at all times is helpful if you love the tactile sensation of writing on paper. But don't write in a journal while you're driving. Please. Pull over first.

What I have found useful from behind the wheel of a car is the ability to dictate ideas into my smartphone to get them into Evernote. Use your online note taking system of choice. Siri is my friend and confidant. Yes, I live in the Apple ecosystem. The Google or Microsoft world is fine too. But remember, even when you're dictating into your phone, you're still being distracted, so please be careful. If at all possible, when a thought pops into your head that you want to capture, pull over in a safe place and talk or write to your heart's content. Who knows, your muse may be giving you the seeds to the next Harry Potter series.

When will you write?

All of your "whens" will be laid out in a schedule later in the Program. But the main point here is to carve out a consistent time to write every day. If all you have is fifteen minutes a day, do that.

The goal is to write. To get this project done, you have to write. Far too often, a project manager will spend months and months planning a project—documenting it from every imaginable direction with umpteen different ways to report on it, and never pull the trigger. The project never gets off the ground. In government speak, it may never be funded and executed. It's placed on the shelf never to see the light of day.

We don't want that happening to your book. Define your writing time, and make it sacred. If you're a parent of young children, it may have to be at 4:00 a.m. When I'm working on a book, I get up at 4:00, get through my routine (more on that later), and hit the keyboard by 4:30.

Where will you write?

Of course, you can write anywhere. But if you can create a personal writing space, it will help to keep you motivated. If you know that you have to be at a certain location at the designated time every day, your writing habit will grow leaps and bounds.

Of course, at 4:00 a.m., it could easily be the dining table if that's what you have to work with. If you don't have space at home, but you can get out, maybe your writing space is at the coffee shop down the street. I don't do it myself, but I've read about studies indicating that the buzz of activity in a coffee shop is actually soothing to the working brain and can improve productivity.

Why are you writing?

Now, there's a question for you. One for the ages, perhaps. Of course, only you know why you write or why you want to write. Here are a few reasons that might fit.

- I write to . . .
- help others
- get stories documented for family and friends
- make money
- therapy
- kill time
- practice typing
- practice handwriting
- brainstorm a process or practice
- change the world

Obviously, this list can go on and on. But there is a quote I'd like you to think about. In her book, *Big Magic*, Elizabeth Gilbert warns us, "Please don't try to help me. I mean it's very kind of you to help people, but please don't make it your sole creative motive because we will feel the weight of your heavy intention, and it will put a strain upon our souls."

So, what does she mean exactly? I'll tell you what I think she means. It is my view that there is only one good reason to write—and that's because you have something to say. If your message reaches someone who needs it at that very moment, and it happens far more often than you may realize, then all the better. You've helped someone. But if you sell me your book and tell me that it is to help me or that is your goal, you've placed a burden on me to be helped. It's a fine line, but don't put that expectation on your readers. Just let them read your message and take from it what they will.

That strategy also relieves you of any responsibility for your readers' takeaway. Again, it's a fine line, but please think about it. Don't assign expectations to your readers. It may heap guilt on them if they don't respond the way they think you want them to.

How will you write?

To discuss how you write, we'll have to cover a few things. Will you write on a computer? Do you like to write with paper and pencil? People still do that by the way. Even top-shelf authors like James Patterson write their books with a pen on a legal pad. Of course, in his case, he has a team that he hands his notes off to, and they transcribe them into a word processor.

In the likelihood that you will end up on a computer in one form or another, which word processor will you use? There are tons available. Here is a short list of the more popular options:

- Microsoft Word (of course)
- Scrivener (my personal favorite)
- Google Docs (great for collaborative writing)
- Ulysses (In case you haven't heard of it, it's a nifty little text editor capable of formatting in Markdown. It's Mac-only at the time of this writing.)
- Pages (Apple's answer to MS Word)

Again, there are tons to choose from. But regardless of your weapon of choice, you will likely have to export your final draft to MS Word in the end for the final steps of the publishing process. That's because MS Word is still the de facto standard in the publishing industry. Your editor likely uses MS Word because of the Track Changes feature it provides to show an author what they've done.

Granted, there are a few editors out there that are willing to edit in your favorite word processor, especially since there are now other options for tracking changes. Google Docs, for example, now has that feature.

In any case, after the interior layout designers are finished, the files used for uploading to your distribution channels will be PDF, Mobi (for Kindle), ePub (for Apple Books), which usually makes it your interior designer's problem. More on that later. Much more.

Pantser or Plotter?

Of course, this is a little outside the context of this chapter, but it's interesting to see how different people fall into these two categories. In his book, *On Writing*, Stephen King discusses the idea of pantsers and plotters. In the extreme, a pantser is one who prefers to write from their gut. This is most often associated with novelists waiting for the muse to tell them where the story goes next. I fall loosely in that category.

A plotter, on the other hand, is one who outlines the book in every detail to the point where the book almost writes itself. Chapters and sections and scenes are listed in great detail before the first word is placed in the manuscript.

The truth is, we probably all fall somewhere in between the two extremes. I usually go into a novel with the end in mind. I see the vivid detail of the closing scene before I begin writing. Of course, that scene may change by the time I finish the book, but it provides me with the motivation I need to get through all of the intermediate scenes to get to "The End."

Some plotters get pretty hardcore about it and insist that any successful novelist has to outline their stories before they write. I've heard these types preach at other novelists about the evil of their ways. But if you are a pantser, rest assured, you are not alone—not by a long shot. Even Stephen King self identifies as a pantser, as do I.

As mentioned earlier that I have a rough idea of the closing scene in my head when I begin writing. But I start writing my main characters early. The further I get into the story, the more these characters start waking me up at four in the morning with the stories *they* want to tell. It's a magical time. Maddening sometimes, but magical. I have to get out of bed, quickly make coffee, and get to my computer to capture the movie racing through my head.

In a trilogy I recently completed, I became such close friends with the protagonist, in the second and third books, I almost forgot to introduce him. I still probably didn't do a very good job of it. I just assumed everyone knew my good friend, Brandon.

Determining the who, what, when, where, why, and how of the work essentially builds an umbrella that covers your book; a priceless tool that keeps you focused and moving forward in your writing. Every journalist knows this. This is a key component of Integration Management.

Planning Data

When planning a book project, it is important to have the mindset of a project manager. Once that big decision to publish is made, there are a few data points to jot down. First, set the launch date. I find it helpful, and often more exciting, to pick a special day; your birthday, someone else's birthday, a special holiday based on the story, etc. It isn't necessary, and I know of no real psychology behind it, but it helps to keep me motivated.

Then, set the target word count based on genre. Don't get too hung up on this. The length you need is the length it takes to tell your story. After you've written a few books in your genre, you'll get a feel for your voice and your audience expectations. Yes, you *will* be writing multiple books, won't you? We'll talk more about book length by genre later.

Once you've decided on the launch date, back up two to three months and mark the final manuscript completion date. Determine if you will use beta readers (highly recommended) and how long they will have to read and comment to your draft. Before that is the time you have available to write. Calculating your writing requirement will be a huge variable based on how often you will write and the number of words you write per session. Adjusting this will adjust your start and completion dates. Project managers call this the critical path. Be realistic. We will discuss more of these details as we go. This initial data is merely to get your mindset working in the right direction, not to finalize your plan.

Launch Day

When preparing to write a book, there are some specific data points you should start out with. Your entire process will be predicated on one specific date: *Launch Day*. Even if you don't plan to publish your book, you should still set a launch date to keep you marching to a deadline. Is there some magic mojo that you need to place on deciding your launch day? Not really. Some will tell you it's best to launch on Tuesday, presumably due to the planning and recovery requirements attached to weekends. I have no data to prove or disprove that.

Of course, it's probably not a good idea to launch on major holidays when your readers' attention is focused elsewhere. All of the new blockbuster movies are coming out on Christmas these days, too, so there's that.

Because the planning and scheduling of your book activities is anchored on launch day, you start there and backup into all of the other milestones necessary to publish the book. We'll get into those details in the Time Management chapter, but for now, here are a few things to consider on your schedule:

- First Draft
- Rewrite or Author Edit
- Beta Reader Inputs
- Editing
- Book Cover Design
- Interior Design and Layout
- Back Cover Copy
- Ancillary Material (workbook, promotional material, etc.)
- Launch Day Planning
- File Uploads
- Publishing

There is much more involved under each of those headings. But all that is only half the fun. The other half, I won't cover in this book because I'm just not an expert . . . yet. That other half is marketing. If you're going to publish, your book is a useless endeavor if people don't know it's out there. Now that you're in the writing business, you have to develop a whole different mindset, one that factors in self-promotion. Because selling isn't selling. Not for us. You'll hear it said in different ways: Selling is sharing. Selling is storytelling. Selling is serving.

Regardless of the context, selling your book is the act of letting people know that it's out there. Cliff Ravenscraft once told me that there could be someone in the world on the brink of self-destruction. But for something you said in your book, their life would have ended, even though your book may have had nothing to do with self-help. We just never know.

I know that's a bit heavy, but don't cheat someone out of the message in your book. Learn to be a marketing ninja. That's what I'm working on.

Word Count (Don't Sweat It! But...)

While you won't know exactly where you'll end up, it's always good to set a word count goal. It's the only way to track progress. And tracking progress is what keeps you motivated. You won't know how close you are if you don't know where you're going, after all.

There are some loose industry standards in this regard. I say "loose" because they are continually evolving with the average reader's attention span. Of course, that means shorter. We'll get into pricing much further down the road, but for now, just know that your word count has nothing to do with the price of your book. So don't stress over that. Here are some of those loose standards as fiction goes, according to CareerAuthors.com:

- Romance: 65,000–80,000 words
- Mystery: 80,000 words
- Science Fiction: 100,000–120,000 words
- Thriller: 90,000–100,000 words
- True Crime: 90,000–100,000 words
- Historical Fiction: 100,000–150,000 words
- Mainstream Women's Fiction: 90,000–100,000 words
- Memoir/Bio: 70,000–90,000 words
- Literary Fiction: 80,000–100,000 words
- Young Adult: 70,000–80,000 words
- Middle Grade: 40,000–50,000 words
- Picture Books: 500–700 words

Technically, according to ManuscriptAgency.com, anything over 40,000 words is considered a novel. A novella is 10,000–40,000 words. These word counts are a guide only because it is what the readers might expect in each of the genres. There are always exceptions. My thrillers, for example, are only 60,000 words and can be read over a rainy weekend.

As nonfiction works go, word count is almost irrelevant. Many experts say they should be over 40,000 words, but these books run the gamut from tiny pamphlets to doorstops of significant tonnage. It is beneficial to become familiar with your audience's expectations and their patience for long dissertations.

Know Thy Audience

Again, don't get panicky over this, but when you know whom you're writing for, it can affect things like word count and even how you write. Many experts refer to this as your avatar. Create the person you are writing for. Know everything about them. As mentioned earlier, demographics are good, but also know their psychographics. More often than not, they are people like you. If you have lost someone close to you and are writing about that experience, you know the person you are writing for has felt that pain. They understand your words. Those who don't get it simply may not be your people.

Know your people. Pick that one person who exemplifies your audience and perch them up on top of your computer, desk, or kitchen cabinet if you're writing at the breakfast table. Write to them. They are your gift from the muse and your motivation.

In the next chapter, we will discuss book proposals in great detail. The book proposal is your project plan. It's where all of this planning data will reside. We've covered the essentials here, but there is much more to learn in order to prepare that proposal. Oh, and don't think that because you are an indie author with no plans to approach an agent or traditional publisher that you're going to get a pass on the book proposal. It's just as beneficial for the author as it is for outside agencies, if not more so.

The Project Plan is Your Book Proposal

As an author, your project plan is known to everyone in the industry as the fateful *Book Proposal*. As an indie author, you might not need to worry with the formatting perfection that you would with outside submissions, but it's a good idea to go through the process in order to understand your book.

There is a lot to think about as you enter the writing process. Most of it has to do with what happens after it's written. If your plan is to sell the book, you need to understand your market; things like price point for your various formats, what others are writing in the genre and how they compare to yours, who your ideal reader is, and what qualifies you to write the piece in the first place. Most importantly, what is the message you want to share? Everything in the book must point to and reinforce that message. You don't want your book to read like the ramblings of a drunken sailor, do you? I don't know. Could be fun.

(Sorry. No offense to sailors. I was one once.)

Rather than go through the myriad disconnected questions you need to answer here, I'll just provide a template. You can take this and format it however you like—or not format at all. The important thing is answering the questions so you can better understand your book. I'll probably say this many times, but if you have things you want to write in your draft manuscript now, do that. There is nothing more important about this process than writing the book. So, first and foremost, sit your butt down and *write*.

A proposal provides a map for you. I'll provide this template for reference. You can get a blank template at TerryStafford.com/resources/pmw.

The Template

BOOK PROPOSAL STRUCTURE

Title Page

    I. The Content

        A. Premise

        B. Unique Selling Proposition

        C. Overview

        D. Manuscript

1. Manuscript Status

2. Special Features

3. Anticipated Manuscript Length

4. Anticipated Manuscript Completion Date

II. The Market

A. Demographic Description

B. Psychographic Description

C. Affinity Groups

D. Competition

III. The Author

A. Background

B. Previous Writing

C. Personal Marketing

Chapter-by-Chapter Synopsis

Sample Chapters

Now, let's go through each part of the proposal. Again, format is not important here if you aren't submitting to agents and publishers. A simple Q&A sheet will work just fine.

The Title Page

Picking a title and subtitle for a book can be like naming a baby. One could argue that you are, indeed, naming a baby. It can be tough. While you don't need to have your title finalized at the outset, you'll need to settle on one before you get your cover designed—certainly before you publish, if that's your goal. Many authors simply begin with a working title in mind in order to keep their thoughts organized around it or to communicate with their team about it. Sometimes it sticks; sometimes it doesn't. Early in the process, you need to sit and brainstorm through some options.

The cover and the title are the first thing a potential buyer will look at. The title needs to be clear and should let the reader know what they are getting. It needs to make a promise or provoke curiosity. This can often be easier with nonfiction than with fiction. With fiction, the title may be referring to a world the potential reader isn't yet familiar with. But go with a working title for now if needed. Many times, the real title will emerge as you write the book.

The same goes with your subtitle. Go with a working subtitle in the beginning so as not to get stuck on a detail and forget to write the book.

The subtitle typically lists the features of the book. Said another way, the title is the *what* and the subtitle is the *how*. Luckily for novelists, fiction books typically don't need a subtitle. Of course, there can be tag lines on the front and back cover of a novel to spark interest, but an actual subtitle isn't necessary. Let's get into the Content section of the proposal.

Premise

The premise states the problem and then proposes your solution. It is a brief statement, usually one paragraph. It can often be easier with non-fiction than with fiction since the existence of a problem and solution is assumed. Here is an example:

Andy Andrews, *The Traveler's Gift*

The Traveler's Gift weaves history with spirituality into a much-needed message of inspiration in this culture of self-promotion. Andrews believes that to be a soulful-led person, you must believe in yourself and the work you are doing. It is a simple but profound spiritual philosophy about how to succeed in the world—easy to understand and to take to heart.

Unique Selling Proposition

This is the value of your book. What can the reader expect to take away from it? What is unique that will help them? It is unique in that it is something your competition cannot or does not offer. It must attract potential customers; in this case, readers. This gets into your marketing. Many, if not most, authors hate the idea of marketing or selling. Look at marketing this way: it's sharing. Nobody will know your book exists unless you share it with them. They need to know the value it provides, or you've allowed them to miss an opportunity to learn and grow with your gift. Don't rob them of that blessing.

Sticking with the Andy Andrews example, *The Traveler's Gift*, here is his USP that provides the benefits of his work.

- After completing *The Traveler's Gift*, readers will (benefits):
- Be encouraged to bravely and successfully begin and finish the journey.
- Take unstoppable action in every area of their lives toward what they want.
- Embrace each day happily and joyously.
- Learn how to become more effective leaders.

  . . . because the book will do the following (features):
- Highlight seven fundamental strategies for creating a successful life.
- Let everyone from all walks of life know that it's okay to experience setbacks, failures, and hardships.

Again, start with your best intentions in mind. The framework or storyline you want to share will likely evolve as you write the book. Andy might have had four fundamental strategies in his features list when he started his book but then added a few more as he wrote the manuscript. He could easily have gone back and changed his USP to say seven instead of four.

Overview

This section of the book proposal might be considered the executive summary. Think through the overall message of the book and describe it here. You could break it into parts of the journey or sections to describe each step you want to lead your readers through.

> Part 1: The environment
> Part 2: The problem or pain point
> Part 3: The cure or solution

Of course, do this only if it makes sense for your book. Break it down in a logical sequence to better explain the overall story in a few paragraphs. This can also pertain to fictional stories. These parts may help you think through the arc of the story.

Manuscript

Most of this section will be evolving since it is essentially the status of the book. Frankly, you would only need to stay on top of this if you were planning to send your book proposal to an agent or editor. You will shed light on the status of your manuscript by answering these questions.

Status: Is it complete? Is it partially done? How many words of the total plan have you written?

Features: Do you have discussion questions at the end? Are there illustrations, graphs, charts? Is there any integrated or ancillary content online?

Word Count: Give your best estimate of the planned total word count. In the absence of more accurate data, 40,000 words is a good target to shoot for. Consider the industry standards provided earlier. But as I mentioned, the trend is toward shorter books that can be consumed in fewer sittings. For whatever reason, it's becoming more difficult for people to commit long periods of time to reading these days. A sad truth.

Completion Date: When will you finish the manuscript? Remember that launch date I mentioned? That's your anchor. The completion date is another major milestone. The time between this milestone and the launch date milestone is the time you will have to get the manuscript through all of the required wickets. But to solve the equation, take the total word count and divide it by your anticipated writing pace. How many words do you plan to write per day? Will you write every day of the week? Three days a week? An easy pace is 500 words per sitting. A range that might be a challenge is 2500 to 5000 words per day, but is doable for the more full-time writer. We'll discuss all of this more in the chapter on Time Management.

Here's an example using one of my books:

Strings of Faith

I.   Manuscript Status: The introduction and sample chapter are completed (both are attached to this proposal).

II.   Special Features: The manuscript will include a story of marriage, friendship, adoption, and the loss of a child. The protagonist puts her dream on hold while dealing with the painful realities of life. But her friends and God lead her back in a way that teaches tremendous faith and what is truly important in life. The moral of the story invokes specific things to consider when recovering from the pain of loss and dealing with people in the process. There will also be questions for discussion at the end of the book that can be used in small group study.

III.   Anticipated Length: 60,000 words

IV.   Anticipated Manuscript Completion Date: August 12, 2016

The Market

Now, let's talk about your audience—all those people that you're writing for. Who is your target audience? And trust me, "everyone" is *not* the right answer. Of course, you want everyone to read your book, but not everyone will. Long story short, if you try to write for everybody, you'll end up writing for nobody.

You can target African American males, ages 35–55, with an interest in finance and football, who identify themselves as Christian, have an affinity for Tony Robbins, and possess a college degree. Pretty specific, right? Pretty amazing.

In the not-too-distant past, large companies paid millions of dollars to advertising firms to create ad campaigns that targeted specific buyers. Odds are, you don't have that luxury. Nor do you need it. When it comes time for the actual marketing of your book, you'll discover just how amazing online tools are now. But you'll also discover that, these days, marketing is more about relationships and less about selling.

This section is about discovering your people. Who needs the value you're providing? Start by identifying the characteristics (demographics) and motivations (psychographics) of your readers. Here are a couple of definitions for you:

Demographics – The characteristics of your readers—the external factors like age, religion, education, location, occupation, etc. Demographics answer the question: "Who would read my book?"

Example: The audience for _____ (your book's title) will be middle to upper-class women between thirty and fifty years old who own their own business or work within organizations that depend on growth for success.

Psychographics – These are the motivations of your readers. Think internal factors like attitudes, values, fear, and drives. Psychographics answer the question: "Why would people read my book?"

Example: The audience for this book is made up of people who are interested in achieving their full potential by taking personal responsibility for their growth and who consider themselves to be lifelong learners. They join groups and courses on a regular basis. Or, the audience for this book is people who have lost a loved one within the last six months.

This is another area that is evolving in today's culture. With many of the nonfiction works coming out today, demographics are playing less of a role in marketing and psychographics are becoming more important.

Novels, on the other hand, may play better into the hands of specific groups of people.

An important thing to consider when developing the psychographics of your ideal reader, is the possibility or even the likelihood that you are writing for people just like you. That should make it a little easier to capture on paper. If you're writing about the pain of losing someone to cancer, it's probably because you've been through it. Your readers are going through it too. Those are your people.

Affinity Groups – People will have a natural affinity for your book based on your identity (who you are) and your topic (what you say). Invest some time in pinpointing these people. The more specific you are, the better. Generalizations like "women" are hard to track and therefore hard to market to. Again, these might be people just like you, but maybe not. Think outside the box this time. For example, there are many other reasons that people might want to identify with you. In the case of losing someone to cancer, maybe your affinity groups consist of caregivers, medical professionals, students, etc.

Instead of identifying simply "women," a better choice might be "subscribers to *Woman's Day*." It can be tracked with names, email addresses, and profiles. This affinity group has a Facebook page of over 290,000 likes and a Twitter account with over 8,000 followers. Here is an example of affinity groups with our friend, Andy Andrews's book, *The Traveler's Gift*:

- People who are multi-level distributors (Amway, New Vision, Mary Kay, etc.)

- Former readers of *Country America* magazine where Andy's articles have been featured
- People who subscribe to the following magazines: *Success, Entrepreneur, Readers Digest, Guideposts, Saturday Evening Post,* and other human-interest publications
- You might even include pictures of the covers of the targeted publications for motivation and reference.

Competition – As it implies, these are other books written in your genre. The easiest way to find these is by perusing Amazon using the search feature. Be careful with this. It's important to know what else is out there, but it can also drive your critical inner-voice crazy. Listen for this self-talk and shut it down:

- "What makes you think you I can write something better than that author?"
- "Who are you to say something on that topic?"
- "You can't add anything that hasn't already been written."

The fact of the matter is, nobody has heard your story in your voice. But it helps to research the similarities and differences between your work and a few of the most closely related books in your genre. You can easily get this information from the Amazon sales page.

- Page count
- Premise (from the book's description)
- Publisher (this can tell you a lot about the general content of the book)
- Pricing

- Popularity (the book's ranking in specific Amazon categories)
- Promotion (Check the Author Page for social media integrations and blog feeds to see how they are promoting their book (and if it's working)

Be careful not to get totally bogged down in this. You can easily reach overkill and get totally distracted from your own work. This is intended to simply give you an idea of what else is out there and how others do marketing. For example, if you are writing a book on leadership, you might research and develop a short list similar to this:

Project Management for Writers (research for this book)

1. David Kadavy, *How to Write a Book*. (Kadavy, Inc., 2018), 48pp, $8.99.

Differentiation – *How to Write a Book* is a short, simple method shared by the author that is extremely oversimplified, but at least gets the reader acclimated to the industry and provides a place to start. It is a very short read with little in the way of specific repeatable processes to develop a workflow for the writing practice. The target audience seems to be the aspiring author, while *Project Management for Writers* is written for experienced writers as well.

Similarities – Just like *Project Management for Writers*, the book attempts to introduce potential writers to the process of writing with a brief introduction into the publishing industry.

You should go on to list two or three more books similar to yours and get clear on what's different. But again, don't allow yourself to get bogged down in this. Your story will always be unique in many ways.

The Author

It's time for you to shine. This can often be more difficult than it sounds. If you haven't done it before, you might look up some resources on how to write a biography. You can find examples on websites like Grammarly, Indeed, YouTube, Writers Digest, and a bazillion others you can find with a simple internet search.

Your book is going to be a reflection of you. So, look in the mirror. Who is this person that is about to go on this journey? The journey of writing may become a time of self-discovery in itself, so don't hesitate to revisit this and edit it once the first draft of your manuscript is complete. But don't delay in writing this. At least the first draft of it.

In this section, you'll address three questions:

1. Who am I?
2. Why am I qualified to write this book?
3. What will I do to market it?

If this gives you pause, welcome to the human race. For one, talking about yourself isn't the easiest thing in the world to do, but you have to learn to present yourself as an author. Go ahead, say it. "I am an author." Not, "I want to be an author," or, "after this book is done, I'll be an author." No. You *are* an author! Okay. Now, stop focusing on yourself and start focusing on your readers. You're answering these questions for them. What do they need to know about you?

When writing this, keep your *why* front and center. If you've written a bunch of books, say so. If you've never written and published before, you can move past that section. We all started somewhere. As you might have figured out by now, this bio is going to evolve throughout the rest of your life. So, don't feel like you're locked into it. I'll use my friend Kary Oberbrunner as an example:

Background: Kary Oberbrunner's purpose and passion is to connect people to a process that ignites their souls on fire. An author, coach, trainer, and speaker, he earned his doctorate in transformational leadership and founded two companies—Redeem the Day, which serves the business community, and Igniting Souls, which serves the nonprofit community. Author of numerous books, Kary is a Founding Partner on the John Maxwell Team. He and his wife, Kelly, are blessed with three amazing children.

Previous Writing: Kary Oberbrunner, a prolific writer, is represented by one of the top agents in the industry, Kathy Helmers of Creative Trust. He has authored five books and is under contract for one more. His publishing portfolio includes the following books: *The Deeper Path* (Baker, 2013), *Your Secret Name* (Harper/Zondervan, 2010), *The Fine Line* (Harper/Zondervan, 2008), *Called* (BMH, 2007), and *The Journey Toward Relevance* (Relevant Books, 2004).

Personal Marketing: Kary has recorded over 100 TV and radio interviews and written a variety of books on topics related to leadership, faith, and personal transformation. He blogs regularly at www.karyoberbrunner.com and has built a large virtual international following via his social media channels. Kary is a creative and committed promoter who proactively markets each of his books. He speaks nationally at businesses, conferences, churches, and campuses; blogs regularly (3–4 times a week); has recorded over 100 radio and TV interviews (including several features on the 700 Club); and has launched comprehensive social media integrated marketing campaigns including fan pages, Twitter lists, blog tours, read-along groups, launch parties, giveaways, sponsorships, and original articles. He collaborates/creates websites for his books (www.yoursecretname.com) and writes scripts for his book trailers.

This is a long-form bio, and you will find yourself needing to cut this down into various shorter lengths. Remember what I said about this being an ever-changing and growing bio? I happen to know this sample bio is outdated. Kary is an amazing entrepreneur who has accomplished much more since that bio was written. You should look him up. Tell him I sent you.

Okay. Now, you do it. Again, whether or not you have all of Kary's credentials, you have a story. Your life is relatable to so many of the people on this planet. Don't keep yourself a secret.

Chapter-by-Chapter Synopsis

Woohoo! You've almost gotten this book proposal thing whipped into shape. But now comes the critical part. The part about the book. This is where your book comes alive. If you are a plotter, this is the fun part. If you are a pantser like me, it might be a little grueling. In any case, you have to think through your book. You've already defined your parts or sections from the overview above, right? Start there. Write those down again in this section of the proposal. Those will be your headings.

Amazon's "Look Inside" feature allows potential purchasers an opportunity to sample the soup. Imagine your chapter titles listed there. Do they attract that reader's attention? They should evoke an emotional response. If those chapter titles are boring, readers will assume your book is boring.

Remember that stories sell. Each chapter will be one of your self-contained stories or illustrations that will lead your reader along through the book. Make sure your chapters flow logically. Also, remember this most popular axiom for authors, especially known among fiction writers. Show don't tell. In this context, use it to provide a taste of what the reader can expect by sharing your chapter outline. But don't serve up the whole meal. You want them to want more.

There are many ways you can provide this synopsis. You can simply list some bullet points or outline style paragraphs. Ask questions to engage the reader. The chapter title must pull the reader into the content of the paragraph. Tag lines can be helpful as well. There are copywriting tricks that you can use to grab attention.

"Do you feel trapped?"

"Why the when is now."

Again, engage the reader. The sequence of steps to create the synopsis is completely up to you and your writing or thinking style. List out the ti-

Project Management for Writers:

tles, go back and fill in the paragraph description, then write the description as you list the titles. Many authors write out the description of the chapter first and see if a good chapter title jumps out at them. The muse works in mysterious ways. Here is an oversimplified example:

Part 1

The Problem

Chapter 1 – It's What's Inside That Counts

Over 80% of the population want to write a book. Only 3% actually do it. A much smaller percentage of those go through with the publishing process. That's a problem.

Chapter 2 – People Need Your Story

You would be surprised at the stories that change lives. Someone in the world is waiting for the story that only you can tell. Too many of these stories are withheld.

Part 2

The Plan

Chapter 3 – Let's Build a Personal Writing and Publishing Process

Chapter 4 – When Do You Know You Are Finished?

Part 3

The Payoff

Chapter 5 – Marketing Your Book to Success

Chapter 6 – What to Do with Those Millions

Again, way oversimplified, but you get the idea. Each chapter synopsis should be a paragraph or two. You'll get a chance to write an entire chapter later.

48

Sample Chapter

If you are an indie author, it probably isn't necessary to actually add the sample chapter. But if the proposal is going outside for any reason, it should include that sample. Editors will typically ask for a sample chapter primarily so they can assess your style for a match or use it to show you what their editing process looks like. They will take your sample chapter and return a sample edit.

If you are looking for an agent, they will certainly need to see your work. For them, you will also need to include an introductory cover letter. Since I'm an indie myself, I have no experience with submitting to agents and publishing houses. Pretty much all of my author friends are indies as well, so even a reference might be difficult. But there are plenty of resources out there to use, if that is your goal.

But hey, you have to write the book anyway, right? So, that sample chapter will be available whenever you need it. Just make sure the sample chapter is the best that it can be. Put the polish on it—just like a résumé for a new job. If you're submitting to an agent or publisher, that's exactly what it is. The entire proposal should be flawless.

Congratulations!

Once you've gotten your proposal done, you have your framework— your project plan. Take a break. Go celebrate. Because when you come back to your writing space, it's time to get down to work—the real work of writing a book. Now you have the breadcrumbs that are going to lead you down your storytelling path.

What if your writing leads you onto another path, taking you away from your plan? Of course, you have a decision to make. There are several options. If you're a pantser, it's wonderful. I live for these moments. Press on! See what's down there.

If you're a plotter, this will likely be a distraction for you. If you need to stay on task, jot the idea down in a file that some call a parking lot. You don't want to forget it, but you have to set it aside for the time being. Perhaps it is the seed of another book. Or maybe you simply go back and add the idea to your proposal as another chapter, or let it play a part in an existing chapter.

What's most important is that you don't allow it to freeze you. Either follow the path, or don't. Write that new branch of the story to see where it takes you, or jot down the idea for later consideration and press on with the plan. But never just blow it off and forget it. Great ideas work hard to find their way to you. At least extend them the courtesy of finding them a home, even if it's just a temporary home.

In the project management world, chasing things down rabbit holes is called Scope Creep. You've developed your project plan, but the further down the road you get during implementation, the more things that may impact your schedule or cost will creep in. What you do to control Scope Creep is called Scope Management. We'll take a look at that in the next chapter.

Planning for Other Content

If you're writing for something other than creating a manuscript for a book, the planning will be different. You aren't going to be troubled with a book proposal if you are simply writing blog posts or creating content for podcasts and websites.

In that case, your project plan will be more like an ongoing content-creation calendar. A strategic plan may simply contain items like the purpose of the content, the publication cycle, word count requirements, etc. In the case of podcasts, they may spawn ancillary writing such as show notes.

In these cases, time blocking will be your friend. Set your calendar up for success. That is the tactical aspect of content planning. If you publish a blog post every Tuesday, for example, back your workflow up to set times for ideation, drafting, editing, graphics, uploading, and publishing. When these times are blocked out to show up automatically on your calendar, it will help ensure that your blog post will be ready when your publishing day comes around. Now let me say a few words about tools.

Writing and Integration Tools

Back to books. As I've said, you don't need to spend a penny to write a book. There are many free tools available like Google Docs or Apple Pages. If you're writing on an iPad, in addition to the free apps Apple provides, you can look at text editors like Ulysses.

Microsoft Word is the standard in the publishing industry, but it isn't free. If you plan to get serious about writing with multiple books, you should make the investment and get Word. A serious author should also consider making an investment in a writer-specific tool like Scrivener. I wouldn't necessarily recommend it for first-time authors or those who only plan to write one book. There is a pretty steep learning curve to take advantage of all the capabilities inside Scrivener.

If you choose to manage an ongoing writing practice, it might be worth looking into a project management or integration application like Asana, Trello, Notion, or, my personal favorite, ClickUp. Again, they all have a learning curve, and it's not worth getting involved in them if your plan is to simply write one book for your business or family.

A mind-mapping tool is great for brainstorming book ideas and drilling down into the details of a specific book idea. There are apps to help with this, or you can simply do it with pencil and paper. The principle behind mind mapping is to capture and explore ideas as they come, in no particular order. Our minds don't generally operate in a linear fashion like one might see in a formal outline.

If you're familiar with the management technique called Post-It Note brainstorming, you understand the basics of mind mapping. First, capture unedited thoughts and ideas for as long as it takes (though, some in a conference room will set a ten-minute timer), then categorize items to start making sense of them. Below is an example of a brainstorming session using a mind-mapping application.

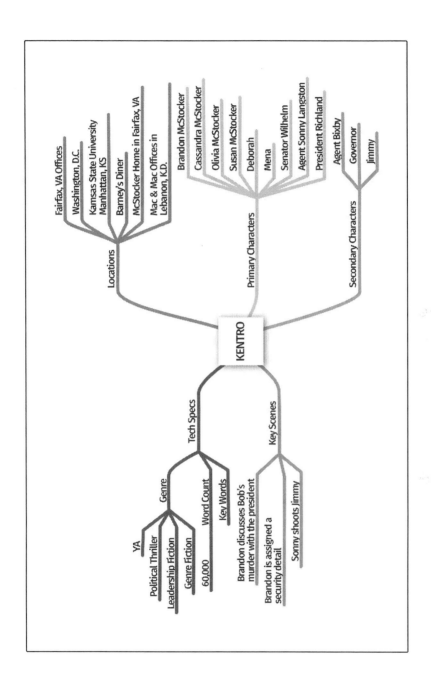

Figure 1 Mind Map

For editing assistance in my work, I use Grammarly. This isn't the end-all solution, and I don't accept everything the tool suggests, but it helps me get my manuscript ready for my editor.

Even though I am an editor myself for many clients, I never allow myself to be the final editor for my own manuscripts.

File Management

If you are just starting out as a writer, you probably haven't thought about file management. While you may wonder what the big deal is when you only have one simple MS Word document in a folder on your computer, the fact is, you're going to end up with all kinds of different files. Consider your research and how you will file it in a way that is easily retrievable. Multiply that by all those books you're going to write.

You should decide early on where you want to save your data. While it may be safe on your computer while you're working on it, you should have multiple backups somewhere offsite, like in a cloud storage facility.

There are many such services to choose from. If you are in the Apple ecosystem, you can save everything on your iCloud Drive. If not, you can use Dropbox or Google Drive. You can also get similar storage services through Microsoft and many other cloud storage companies.

Once you've determined where you will do your file management, develop a file structure that makes sense to you. My top-level folder is always the title of the book. Under that, I have a Drafts folder that contains progress copies of my early manuscripts; a Covers folder that contains my cover ideas, clips of images, and proposed covers provided by my designer; and an Ancillary data folder for things like early drafts of the back-cover copy, workbook ideas, random support documents, etc.

Then I add a folder under the book title folder called Final Files. That folder contains another folder called Interior Files. That is where the final files from my layout designer go. My designer provides me with .pdf, .mobi, and .epub files for uploading to various distribution sites. You want to make sure you know exactly where they are so you can get to them easily.

Also, under the Final Files folder, I have a folder called Final Covers. There, I save the final eBook cover and the cover spreads formatted for Amazon KDP and Ingram Spark (if you choose to use their services). The template requirements are different for each format, and your cover designer should be well aware of those requirements. Your cover designer may also provide promotional images using the cover images. You can save those images there as well. But you might want to save actual promotions for the book in a separate folder since you might be accessing those long after your book is published.

In the beginning, my files ended up all over the place. I felt like I couldn't find anything when I needed it. Don't put yourself in that position. Create your system structure early. If you've been writing a while but are still unorganized, take the time to create your file management system now. You already know the problems misplaced files can cause.

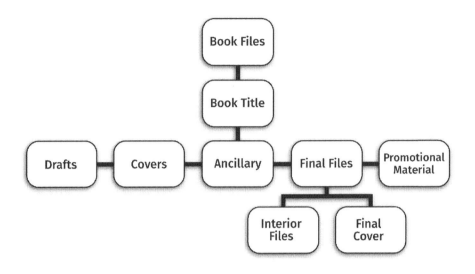

Figure 2 Sample File Management Structure

Even as you write, you should be backing up your files. In fact, at the end of each writing session, it would behoove you to save a new backup copy. Then if anything goes wrong, the worst case would be that you lose a day of work and not the entire manuscript.

One of the beauties of Scrivener is that during the creation process, you can keep all of your research files, like photos, website links, and other documents, within your Scrivener project. Then it's all contained in one file when you save and back up the project. Scrivener also saves a backup to your selected backup location whenever you close the program. Very handy, not to mention safe.

Most authors I know only use Scrivener for the first draft and perhaps a rewrite before compiling the manuscript out to a MS Word document. However, the program does allow you to compile the manuscript out to a finished eBook or straight to a formatting application like Vellum. To be sure, that skips a whole lot of steps in the quality publishing workflow.

Those capabilities may be perfect for creating your own publications for a classroom or to share with family and friends, but if you plan to publish your work through a distributor, you need to use an editor and professional designers.

2.

SCOPE MANAGEMENT

What is Scope Management?

According to the PMI, project scope is the work required to output a project's deliverable. Change happens, and project Scope Management includes the process to manage scope changes and make sure the project will still come in on time and within budget. Scope is often defined by a work breakdown structure, and changes should take place only through formal change control procedures within that structure.

The work breakdown structure has no real value or application in a writing practice, so we'll just leave that here. In fact, Scope Management in general has very limited application to the writing practice except in terms of content and marketing.

For our purposes here, let's describe scope as the intended topic of the work—everything that goes into the document to get the project to its intended end. For writers, the scope can often be described as the breadth or depth of the piece to be written and the tasks required to write it. There has to be a line drawn either way.

For example, if an author writes a book about building a house, the scope of the content must be limited because the breadth of details required in information about building a house is enormous. Each chapter can be focused on one discipline, like concrete foundation, framing carpentry, plumbing, electrical, finish carpentry, windows and doors, painting, etc. But the detail to which these disciplines can be discussed in one chapter of one book is limited to the space available.

Each of these disciplines have volumes of how-to books on the market. The scope of all that must be done to build a house requires that one book of such unlimited breadth must be limited in depth. If, however, a book was written about residential plumbing, the breadth is limited in favor of the depth into the subject.

The scope is defined by the breadth and depth of the content. You can write an article on the United States Constitution, or you can write an article on the Second Amendment. Same topic, different scope.

So, what does all of this mean to the writing practice? You have to manage the scope in order to avoid something called Scope Creep.

Scope Creep

Scope Creep is what can happen when you get distracted from the main task at hand. When you have a job to do around the house, let's say you want to do something as simple as changing the lightbulb in a bedroom ceiling light fixture; that is the scope of your project. Simple, right?

You go to the garage to get a step ladder and replacement bulb. The ladder is hidden behind a mountain of boxes, and you discover the box of replacement bulbs is empty. You decide to deal with digging the ladder out after you return from getting light bulbs at the local hardware store.

While you're in town getting light bulbs, you determine that it is a good opportunity to stop at the grocery store and pick up some buns and ground beef to throw some burgers on the grill later. An hour later, you return to your house, get the food supplies put away, and return to the garage to retrieve the ladder.

While moving boxes out of the way, you discover that your golf cubs were buried under them and remember that you haven't played in a while. You pull the cell phone from your hip pocket and call your friend, Ernie, to see if he would like to set up a tee time. After shooting the breeze for a while, you invite him and his family over for supper in the back yard.

After hanging up, you continue to move boxes and try to stack them in a way that makes better sense—in the corner, out of the way. You end up organizing the garage for two hours before finally returning to the task at hand, which is retrieving the ladder.

We'll leave out the part about misplacing the box of lightbulbs during the reorganizing and simply grab the ladder and lightbulbs and move back to the bedroom to finally change the bulb. That, my friend, is Scope Creep. It's how a fifteen-minute task turns into an all-day affair. We all experience it way too often.

It can also happen when writing a book. If you're writing that book about plumbing, you could easily start discussing the importance of framing walls for plumbing and then find yourself going down the rabbit hole of framing concerns—how to install a pocket door in limited-space bathrooms, etc.

Scope Creep is different than making a conscious change in the scope. If you change your mind about the content of a book and decide to add a couple more chapters, that is a change in scope. Scope Creep can certainly lead you to making that conscious effort, but know that you have to make an effort to stay focused and stay true to the project you set out to complete, if for no other reason than to keep your audience content.

If a reader picks up a book on residential plumbing and finds himself thumbing through pages and pages of framing illustrations, he will likely close the book and put it back on the shelf.

Keep your topic focused to avoid Scope Creep.

3

TIME MANAGEMENT

What is Time Management?

Time management may very well be the most recognizable aspect of what we all know as project management. When we think of Time Management, we think of either a schedule or calendar. Managing the time we have is critical to the successful completion of any writing project. You have to ensure that your writing time is given a prominent place in your life's priorities. If you've heard it once, you've heard it a thousand times. Each of us has only 168 hours in a week.

We all have a list of things to put on our plate to be accomplished each week. If you are a parent, you are also carrying the schedule demands of your children, which only get heavier as they grow into teens. That doesn't mean it isn't doable. It just means there is a lot to do.

Making sure important things don't fall through the cracks can be an art unto itself. One of my commanding officers in the Navy once told me that things are always going to fall through the cracks. The secret of a skilled leader is consciously selecting which things.

So, there's always something. Among all of the "important" things in your life, you have to decide what is important enough to actually get done. Writing requires a mindset. If you want to be an author, you have to nurture the mindset of an author. Make writing a priority.

Even if you can set aside fifteen minutes a day, you can make significant progress on your writing project. Of course, it will take longer than it would if you could write for an hour or more every day. But you will still see progress, and you will still reach the end. It's not a race.

Lay Down a Habit

Anchoring a writing habit is much easier once you have a defined writing space and have carved out a time to write. Again, not absolutely required, but it makes things so much easier. Look for habit-stacking opportunities. In his book, *Atomic Habits*, James Clear describes habit stacking like this: "Some of the best ways to build a new habit is to identify a current habit you already do each day, and then stack your new behavior on top. This is called stacking." It makes it easier to remember and accomplish the new habit.

For example, if you choose to write for thirty minutes every morning, perhaps you can tie it to something you already do every morning. State it something like this: "Every morning after I put on the coffee, I will sit at the table and write into my story journal for fifteen minutes, pour a cup of coffee, and write for another fifteen minutes." Get it? Habit stacking. After a while, coffee won't even taste right without writing during that first cup.

If you've ever been a cigarette smoker, you know exactly how that goes. I know when I quit smoking, I had to quit drinking coffee for a while. Those two habits were too closely tied together to try to eliminate one without the other. In that context, one might describe the antithesis of habit-stacking as eliminating triggers.

Start small and build. Perhaps you start by writing fifteen minutes every morning at the kitchen table. Once that habit is established, maybe after a month, you can move to your new desk in the living room and write there for fifteen minutes each day. Then, increase the time to thirty minutes each weekday and one hour on Saturdays. After a couple months of that, your book is taking shape, and you may be just motivated enough to convert your guest room into an office and move that new desk in there. You finally have a permanent writing space and a permanent writing time.

If you hold off on writing until you have a permanent space and plenty of time, you may never start writing. In five years, you'll look up and find yourself still wishing you could write a book.

Strategic Planning

There are two aspects of Time Management when it comes to your writing practice. At the strategic level, it's a matter of laying out the activities that need to occur in order to complete a manuscript. For our purposes here, completing a manuscript assumes that it will meet professional publishing standards or expectations.

There are two methods for setting this strategic level timeline. Forward pass scheduling and backward pass scheduling. In forward pass scheduling, you establish a start time, like today, then lay out tasks from to-day, linking all of the dependencies together to determine when you can launch.

In backward pass scheduling, you set a launch date, and then work back-ward through the dependent activities to determine the latest date on which the project must begin.

1. Here are the steps involved in setting up your strategic writing plan:

    *   List all tasks required to complete the project.
    *   Brainstorming ideas
    *   Outlining book chapters or principles
    *   First draft written
    *   Research conducted
    *   Second draft
    *   Manuscript out for editing
    *   Back-cover copywriting
    *   Book cover design
    *   Interior layout design
    *   Proofreading
    *   Final layout editing
    *   Upload files to distribution channels
    *   Continued promotion (while marketing is not within the scope of this book, if publishing is the end goal for your writing practice, promotion should begin ahead of launch and requires a specific set of steps that should be included in your schedule.)

2. Assign a likely duration to each task.

   * For example, first draft, 60 days; second draft, 10 days; editing, 2 weeks, etc. Work this out with your service providers.

3. Set the dependencies between tasks.

   * This is typically a finish-to-start relationship; i.e., Task A must be complete before Task B can begin.
   * It might also be a start-to-start relationship; i.e., Task B can begin when Task A begins.
   * Then there may be variations on this relationship, such as Task B can start two weeks after Task A has started. This is moving into the geekiness of project management, so don't be too concerned about all that.
   * If there is no dependency at all, both tasks can be accomplished concurrently. For example, your book cover design can be done while the manuscript is being edited. One does not necessarily depend on the other. However, both must be complete before the upload milestone.

4. If you assume a project's start date is today, you should then be able to determine your earliest launch date.

5. Set your desired launch date and work backward to determine the latest end date of each task, again considering all of the dependencies.

6. The difference between your earliest start date (today) and your latest start date (the latest date you can begin and still meet the desired launch date) is the slack time you will have available for slips and modifications to the schedule.

7. All activities that must be done on time to meet the launch date are known as being on the critical path.

    •   The book cover can be done any time and therefore is not on the critical path. But if the editor is late, the entire project could slip, so editing is on the critical path.
    •   The value in knowing your critical path is that it helps to keep your focus on the things that may delay your book launch and differentiate them from the things that can be put on the back burner if necessary (for the time being).
    •   This is just a handy little tool. Don't let the concept bog you down. As you might imagine, if you ignore an activity long enough, it will become a critical path activity.

Now that your book strategy is spread out on a schedule, you can go back and fine-tune the launch date in your book proposal if you need to.

You can also clearly see that big time-block called Write First Draft. That means you have work to do—hands down, the most critical piece of the entire project. You have to *write*.

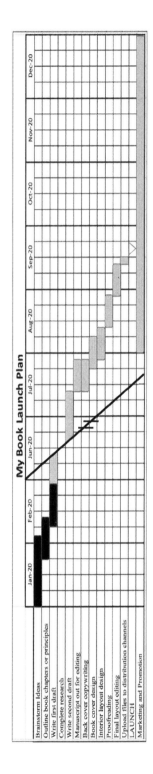

Figure 3 Sample Book Launch Plan

Tactical Scheduling

Tactical scheduling is the act of setting up your writing to-do list. Specifically, this means sitting down with your calendar and plugging in critical milestones (due dates) from your strategic plan and blocking out specific times for the writing. The very first thing you do is schedule your launch date on your calendar.

When I refer to "your calendar," I mean whatever tool you use, whether it be Google Calendar, Apple Calendar, Outlook, an app on your mobile device, or the paper calendar hanging on your refrigerator. Whichever one you pay attention to. They all have essentially the same features. Well, except the one on your fridge doesn't send alerts.

Setting your launch date simply means adding "Launch [book title]" to an all-day event on the date you selected from your strategic plan.

After that, whether you choose to add some or all of the interim milestones, like "Manuscript to Editor" in your calendar or in a more comprehensive project management tool like ClickUp or Asana, that's completely up to you based on how you manage your life.

The main purpose for this tactical scheduling is to get your writing time clearly visible in your life's plan. From your strategic plan, at least note the next step—when you must have the manuscript to your editor. We'll discuss your team and their specific requirements in more detail in subsequent chapters.

Once you know when you need to have your manuscript compete (for the editor), you know how many weeks you have to write. Take the anticipated word count from your book proposal and determine how many words per week you're going to have to write. An example: 40,000 words ÷ 8 weeks = 5,000 words per week.

Then you can determine how to block out that time. You will have to know yourself and your writing endurance. If you're like most of us, you probably won't want to sit and write 5,000 words in one sitting. On the other hand, you may not realistically be able to write every day. Even if you could, it's still 715 words per day.

Maybe you can only realistically write three days per week— Monday, Wednesday, and Friday, at rate of 500 words per hour. That's over 1,600 words per day if you write for a little over three hours. Frankly, that still doesn't sound very realistic to me—at least not on a consistent basis. It may be perfectly realistic for someone who is extremely motivated to get a book out. Perhaps you're willing to do anything to have a family history book complete and ready to give to your daughter on her wedding day. To that author, 1,600 words per day may be perfectly reasonable.

If your math keeps painting you in a corner, it may cause your writing to bring you stress rather than the joy it should bring. It's probably time to reassess your strategic plan and give yourself a more reasonable launch date.

Let's review a few factors to consider:

- Know your pace. If you are a beginner at this, try to become familiar with your writing pace. Perhaps track your journaling a little closer or start doing morning pages, a writing and journaling method introduced in Julia Cameron's book, *The Artists Way*. It's important to know how many words per hour you can write on average.

- Know how many hours per week you can write. It may be every day for an hour. It may be every Saturday morning for two hours. It may be thirty minutes on weekday mornings while making coffee.

- From there, calculate how many hours per week you can write comfortably. I say comfortably because, remember, it's a marathon, not a sprint. You have to be able to maintain the pace.

- Revisit your time to write 40,000 words (or whatever your estimated word count is from your book proposal).

- Remember, you will need to have at least one more pass, probably more, for your rewrite or self-edit. This will go faster than the first draft but give yourself time for this before it's due to the editor.

Now, reset that editor's manuscript due date and reevaluate all of the tasks required to reach the launch date. This may take a couple trips back and forth between your strategist hat and your tactician hat, but once you've set your timeline, your schedule will be much easier to manage—certainly less stressful. Now you can enjoy the ride.

I know I've made a big deal of getting your weekly calendar set up. We all know things are going to happen to pull the rug out from under you. We often say, "If you want to make God laugh, lock in a plan." Even the great warrior and 34th US President, Dwight D. Eisenhower, is often quoted as saying, "Plans are worthless, but planning is everything."

Try to keep your writing up the best you can. Keep your moving average consistent. Maybe you can establish Saturday as a makeup day. If you have to miss one of your writing days during the week, make it up with the additional thirty minutes on Saturday morning. I do that often myself.

As with anything in life, unexpected things happen. There are certain things you know that you don't know, like whether or not your cover designer's mother will have a stroke requiring your designer's full attention. Then there are things you simply don't know you don't know, like . . . well, I don't know. The unknown unknowns.

It's like not knowing which questions to ask. Even worse, not knowing which questions not to ask. Huh?

I digress.

Let's get back to your calendar. I think you get the point. Once you know how many words you have to write and self-edit, and you know how long you have to do it, set your hours-per-week requirement, and block out your writing time.

"I will write for one hour every Monday, Wednesday, and Friday, at 5 a.m. on my laptop computer at the dining room table and will complete 1,500 words per week."

For what it's worth, there is no better feeling than to lift your head from writing one morning and discover you are 5,000 words ahead of schedule. It might be tempting to allow it to slow you down. You can make a better choice. Rejoice, and keep writing.

Now, schedule it! More importantly, do it! What's the most important aspect of writing a book? The answer lives in the question: writing.

4.

COST MANAGEMENT

What is Cost Management?

Cost Management is exactly what it sounds like. In order to end up with a professional-quality book at the end of your project, you should budget for at least the bare essentials. Please understand; there is a price to be paid for quality. But to be clear, don't allow any of what I write in this chapter to deter you from writing your book. It costs you nothing to write except time and a little brain power.

We'll discuss Quality Management in the next chapter. But here, we need to at least discuss expenses. Here is a list of things you should budget for:

- Book cover design
- Editing
- Proofreading
- Copywriting (back cover and ancillaries)
- Proof copies and initial supply

If you are a beginning writer, there may be some initial outlay of costs for tools, office supplies, and any office equipment you may choose for your writing space (if it isn't the dining room table). I won't include any of that here since these aren't considered direct project costs. Of course, if you consider your writing to be your business, and you should, you must absolutely discuss these expenses with your accountant for tax purposes and track them accordingly.

Book Cover Design

There is a pretty wide spread of potential costs associated with the design of your book cover. Often, this expense falls toward the end of the writing process. You don't actually need to have the cover completed until it's time to go to print.

Having said that, I enjoy getting my covers done at the beginning of the project. At least as soon as the title, subtitle, and design concept are nailed down. I do it early because I like to see it in front of me to keep me moving. It's a heck of a motivator. That's why I mention it first among your writing expenses.

On the other hand, it can be a bit risky to do it early. It would be very easy toward the end of your writing to discover that you have strayed so far from your initial outline and concept that your cover no longer makes sense.

Covers are funny things in that regard. On my last novel, *Left Coast Left*, I was so moved by one of the covers proposed by my designer, I selected it almost immediately, even though it depicted a scene that had nothing to do with the story. It took my breath away. Not so much because of the beauty, though it was certainly beautiful, but because of the emotional response it demanded. "Holy crap!" was mine. I wanted it so badly, I added an entirely new chapter in a logical place within the storyline to make it work. It tied everything together brilliantly, if I do say so myself. And yes, it motivated me to keep writing. It drove me to get that story written as quickly as I could.

So, what about cost? As I mentioned earlier, it's a broad category. You could do it yourself for no investment at all beyond your time. But unless you are a trained designer with specific experience in book covers, I would strongly suggest that you hire a professional. A mistake here will certainly spell disaster. There is nothing more important in selling a book than its cover.

In the early days of your writing career, I would suggest a minimum budget of $300 to $500 dollars. If you can afford it, or perhaps later in your writing journey, you should consider leveling up to a higher-end designer in the $1,500 to $2,500 range.

Editing

Editing can easily be considered the most important aspect of publishing any book, cover notwithstanding. It should never be relegated to your English teacher friend who lives down the street, or Uncle Ralph who your mother insists is a "really smart guy." Not to say English teachers can't be good editors, but it's a very different skill.

Editing is something you should never attempt to do yourself. Of course, after the first draft, you have a responsibility to do what is commonly referred to as a rewrite or revision, though seldom do you actually rewrite everything. It's an initial self-edit. You may read through a couple more times to do more self-editing until you are comfortable enough to let it go. Grammarly is a helpful tool during this self-edit phase, but be careful: just as with Microsoft Word's grammar checker, many of its suggestions are wrong.

When it comes time for that final edit, as scary as it is, it must always be done by an expert who is not you. I'm an editor myself and have had many clients, but I never do the final edit of my own work. Never. I've never even been tempted to. I mentioned it earlier, but it's worth saying it again. "He who represents himself has a fool for a client." It certainly holds true for editing your own writing. You have become too close to the material and your brain has learned to overlook mistakes and jump over gaps that exist. Hire it out.

So, what can you expect to budget for professional editing? Again, this can vary, depending on the experience and demand for the editor. Very few editors charge by the hour. It's simply too difficult to provide a job estimate. It is normal for an editor to charge by the word since it is easy to see a word count at the bottom of a Microsoft Word document.

Cost may range from $0.02 per word for a fairly new editor, up to $0.06 per word for a highly experienced editor who is in demand. For a typical mid-range 50,000-word book, that would be $1,000 to $3,000 for copy editing. Line editing and developmental editing can be double that.

If you are just starting out, don't discount the value of the newer editor. They can do good work for you. But it's always a good idea to get referrals. You should always make it a point to get to know other authors, especially in your genre. This is a perfect example of why those relationships are so important. Be careful and look at editor reviews and experience. You are welcome to reach out to me for help if you get stuck. Also, I strongly recommend Jennifer Harshman's book, *Find a Real Editor: Avoiding the Posers and Scammers*. She walks you through the process in great detail.

It's important to find the right editor for your market. If your market is the United States, it's best to find an editor familiar with American English or even varying American dialects. That may sound obvious, but it's important to understand that the writing rules in the UK, for example, have fairly significant differences from those in the US.

As an editor in the US myself, I have had the pleasure of editing manuscripts for writers in the UK, so it is absolutely possible, but it slows things down considerably. The standard style guide for the US trade publication market is *The Chicago Manual of Style*. Once an editor's brain is wrapped around that standard (or any other), it becomes a bit of a challenge to break from it. Not a showstopper but a consideration.

Did I mention that hiring an editor is important? Please don't skip this step.

Proofreading

It's often considered editing, but it actually requires a different technique than editing. And for the same reasons you don't edit your own work, your editor should not be your proofreader. You need fresh eyes on the work for this step in the writing process. We will discuss how the proofreader affects quality in the next chapter. I personally leave my proofreading up to my editor, but that's because I know she farms it out to another member of her team who hasn't seen the manuscript. Or, if she had another member of her team do the editing, she might proofread it herself.

You can expect to pay much less for a proofreader than for an editor. I also proofread for clients, and I always anticipate that the heavy lifting has been completed before I get the manuscript. Proofreading demands that the book be in its final form, i.e., after the interior layout is complete and the PDF is available. This ensures that everything flows as it will when it's between the covers. Of course, some say proofreading should be done prior to layout so corrections can be made using the Track Changes feature in MS Word. That is not actually proofreading; it's another, lighter round of copyediting. The layout process itself causes some errors to be introduced, and those are among the things a proofreader finds and corrects. To each his own, but I would consider going over it prior to layout to be an invitation to perpetual editing.

I do find errors when proofreading, but by this point, they should be few, and I ignore issues that aren't glaring mistakes. I typically log the location of the error by page and paragraph and a change "from" and "to" statement for the author. They can then provide that log to their interior designer to make the corrections. Interior layout designers will often provide the author with their own Correction Log form when they deliver the first PDF file for proofreading.

You might expect to pay in the neighborhood of $0.01 to $0.025 per word for proofreading. So, for that 50,000-word book, you're looking at $500 to $1,250. Again, if you are a beginning writer, you should be just fine at the lower end of that spectrum as long as you're getting referrals or references.

Copywriting

You will likely be tempted to forgo the expense of a copywriter. Don't. A good copywriter is worth their weight in gold. You should try to find a copywriter experienced in the publishing industry to create your back-cover copy. This is often called the blurb or your book description.

Think about your own experience when you shop for books. The cover is what gets your attention. You look at the title. If it piques your interest, you turn it over and look at the back to see what it's about. Often, you won't even finish reading that description before you put it back on the shelf. That's how important a well-written back cover is to the buying process.

The back-cover copy is both an art and a science that requires very specific training that one might acquire at a traditional ad agency. So, I won't even attempt to provide any actual training in the subject here. But good copywriting has so many subtleties, like sentence length, white space, and emotion-packed words, it just isn't worth trying to pull it off yourself. Unless, of course, you are indeed a trained copywriter. Get some referrals from those author friends of yours, and find a good copywriter.

As with others, this is a skill that is all over the map as pricing goes. Above all other disciplines, this is one where a referral is most important. You might expect to pay anywhere from $150 to $1,500. The skill required of a copywriter is unique in that they are not going to read your entire manuscript to come up with a blurb.

They must be skilled at pulling the information from you and turning what you say into a gripping purpose for the book. Think about what you are going to tell the copywriter about your book. Again, they are trained at pulling this information from you, but at least think about it.

If you were to write the book description yourself, you would likely try to summarize what the book is about. In the case of describing it to your copywriter, that's fine. But it's certainly not what the back cover is. Your copywriter will take that description and turn it into a package of gripping sales copy. They might even provide you with some twee-table quotes or one-liners you can use when promoting your book on social media.

Trained copywriters think of things that you and I could never imagine. You might even say they see the world differently. They keep up with the latest trends in what gets people's attention in a noisy world. Even as I write this, I'm thinking I should be using a copywriter in more of what I do.

Proof Copies and Initial Supply

If you choose to publish your book through distribution companies like Amazon KDP or Ingram Spark, you will have an opportunity before they go on sale to purchase a proof copy at cost so you can hold it in your hand to check quality and do a final read-through of the content.

I highly recommend that you schedule the time to do this. It will add a couple weeks to your schedule, but it's well worth it. It's a major pain to have to fix anything at this point, but still, you don't want glaring flaws to go out to your readers.

After you finalize and release the book sale, purchasing copies of your own copies for sales or giveaway is a personal choice. The printers offer author pricing so you can get them at cost. My friend and mentor, Honorée Corder, suggests that giving your books away like candy is an excellent strategy for getting your name and message out into the world.

It's difficult for me to suggest a budget for this line item, but I estimate under five dollars each for your proof copies. That would be a paperback proof from Amazon KDP and a paperback proof from Ingram Spark and a little higher than that for a hardcover proof if you also chose that option from Ingram.

If you want a box of 100 paperbacks available for giveaway, then budget the same author price or $500. At this writing, the KDP price for author copies is between $3 and $4 for most books, so check in with them (and Ingram) for a more accurate budget.

Summary

Service	Estimated Cost
Book Cover Design	$600 – $2500
Editing	$1000 – $3000
Proofreading	$500 – $1250
Copywriting	$150 – $1500
Proofs and Copies	$10 – $1000 (for the sake of estimating, but a highly individual business decision)
Total Budget	$2260 – 9250

In this scenario, you will likely be aiming somewhere between the two extremes. If you're just starting out, perhaps you should lean toward the lower end. If you're already doing well in the publishing space, you should naturally gravitate toward the higher end of the scale.

It is worth repeating that this budget exercise should not stand in the way of your writing. However, if you intend to publish, you don't want to skimp on quality and allow your hard work to be relegated to the heap of far too many subpar books lying in Amazon's ratings scrap pile.

So, let's talk more about quality.

5.

QUALITY MANAGEMENT

What is Quality Management?

Anyone can write a manuscript, throw a cover on it, and call it a book. In fact, it would seem that many authors have done just that on Amazon, paying no attention to the quality of the work.

It's important that authors pay close attention to quality when releasing their message to the world. Critics of indie authors, typically those who are dependent on many layers of the traditional publishing machine, generally throw their darts at the lack of technical skill of indie authors. The major difference between traditionally published books and independently published books has, until recently, been the lack of attention to detail.

Don't fall into the *easy* trap. It makes us all look bad. There are many reasons to decide not to take the traditional publishing route in favor of being an independently published author. Getting through the gatekeepers and beyond the freakishly long time it takes to get published are what I consider the low-hanging fruit of the decision tree. Those are good reasons to self-publish. But getting past the high standards set by traditional publishers should not be one of the reasons. Readers have grown to expect high quality in the books they read.

Fortunately, over the last decade, indie authors have begun paying very close attention to detail resulting in published works that are indistinguishable from those released by the "Big Five" publishing houses.

If you simply can't afford the resources necessary to achieve a high-quality product, my advice would be to wait. Focus on the writing, and find ways to save the funds needed to do it right.

Why Quality Matters

So, what's the big deal? The content is the important part, right?

Well, yes. If the potential reader ever gets that far. For many years, consumers considered self-published books to be associated with vanity presses who released anything if they were paid enough. Everyone assumed poor quality and generally steered clear of them. You never saw these books on the shelves of any reputable bookstore.

Since those days, however, the industry has changed. Authors have taken it upon themselves to work around the bloated and slow-moving publishing houses to get their message out on their own terms. As soon as indie authors started paying attention to quality, ignoring the rules put in place by behemoth trad publishers and agencies, publishing houses began dropping like flies.

Because big-box bookstores were a captive audience for traditionally published books, they too began dropping like flies. Of course, the online reader market brought on by the likes of Amazon Kindle, Barnes and Noble Nook, and others helped hasten their demise.

Where I live, the nearest bricks and mortar bookstore, Barnes and Noble, is over an hour away by car. And it's the only big-name bookstore in the region.

Having said all that, it was the traditional publishers that set the standard for quality in the industry. And it cannot be ignored. Consumers now purchase books with high expectations.

The first thing a consumer sees is the cover—one cover among thousands inside countless categories and genres. If a cover captures their attention, they will pick it up and flip it over (this is assuming we're at a brick-and-mortar bookstore, of course) to read the back cover. If they're still interested, they will open the book and skim the Table of Contents and perhaps a little of the introduction and chapter one. If they are looking at it online, they will look at the photos of the cover and use the Look Inside feature if they're on Amazon.

As a performing musician, I often heard that as long as the intro to a song was solid and everyone ended together, you're good to go. Anything good in the middle is gravy. In a sense, it holds true with books as well. But, while a strong cover and a compelling back-cover blurb might get the book into the shopping cart, it doesn't end there. The last thing you want is for the reader to slam the book closed out of boredom or disappointment after the first couple of chapters. Statistically, it happens more often than not.

The secret of writing a good book is the ability of you, the author, to keep the reader's interest from beginning to end. The front cover must lead the reader to the back cover. The back cover must lead the reader to the Table of Contents or the first paragraph of the first chapter. Each paragraph must then lead the reader to the next paragraph. The last paragraph in each chapter must lead the reader to the next chapter. Ideally, when the reader is finished reading the book, they will want to read more of your books. And yes, with your newly organized writing practice, you'll be set up to write more books. I have faith in you.

That is why quality is so important. Whether or not you choose to publish your work to the general public, you're writing it for a purpose. Even if the intent is to share a story with your family, they deserve your respect and commitment to a high-quality product. Let's give it to them.

Where to See Quality

As we just discussed, quality is needed throughout the book. Let's start where the consumer starts.

The Cover

You may not realize it, but covers are genre-specific. You probably know it without even realizing it. A nonfiction book has a certain look. A fiction cover is completely different. In fact, genres within fiction have their own look. The cover of a romance novel has a very different look than the cover of a political thriller. A cover that doesn't match the story inside can be terribly disappointing to the reader—even deceptive. Never ever try the bait-and-switch tactic with readers. Your Amazon reviews will reflect your deception immediately.

An expert cover designer knows the difference between these genres and keeps up with industry trends. It would behoove any author to seek the expertise of a professional cover designer and not merely a good graphic designer.

Back-Cover Copy

Contrary to the beliefs of some inexperienced authors, the blurb you see on the back cover is not a summary of what's inside. The back cover is sales copy specifically crafted to retain the interest of the reader and get them inside the book.

Just as the purpose of a résumé is to get an interview, not a job; a back-cover blurb is not to sell a book; it's to get the reader inside. Again, writing sales copy is both an art and a science. Unless you are trained and experienced in copywriting, it is best left to the experts. Less-than-stellar work here can leave you in the lurch.

Front Matter

When a reader begins thumbing through the first several pages of an unfamiliar book, they are looking for indications of both content and quality. For this reason, I suggest leaving acknowledgments in the back of the book. Those are usually very boring to the reader, so why put them through it in the front matter? Droning on about all of those faceless people who helped you along the way is certainly important to you and those you are referring to. I'm sure they enjoy seeing their name in your book and appreciate your acknowledgment, but don't expect your average reader to be interested.

The Table of Contents is a reflection of the chapters in the book and what they are about. For that reason alone, it's worth the effort to make sure your chapter titles are worthy of that attention. So even chapter titles should provide a hook.

The first paragraph or two of the Introduction, if you have one, is critical. The same goes for the first paragraph of the first chapter. Whether fiction of nonfiction, the first chapter in any book must begin in the middle of a story. Opening with an action scene can grip the reader from the outset. For example, I opened my novel, Kéntro, with a man running down the corridor toward a conference room. Why? Because right off the bat, the reader is wondering what's going on.

In a nonfiction book, you might open with one of your anecdotes that will immediately resonate with the reader. In any case, opening the first chapter with endless backstory and introductory monolog is the kiss of death. The reader, with a disappointed grimace and the shake of the head, closes the cover and places the book back on the shelf, either literally or, in the case of an eBook, figuratively.

A Word on The Craft of Writing

This book isn't about the craft of writing because it is such a vast topic, and there are already tons of books and courses available on the subject. I consume them on a regular basis. You can never know too much about your craft.

But I will say there is nothing that can distract a reader from your story as quickly as poor writing. Your ability to tell a story can be greatly hampered by your inability to do it with a reasonable grasp of the English language and proper syntax.

This is just one reason that any writer should have their work professionally edited regardless of their own level of expertise and experience. I, for one, would never publish a book without the manuscript first being vetted by both an editor and a proofreader, and I do both of those myself professionally for other authors. We simply get too close to the story to do our own editing. I know, I know. I've said that already. Don't be surprised if I say it again.

So why is all of this craft stuff so important? It's all about flow. Getting from one word to the next, one sentence to the next, one paragraph to the next, and one chapter to the next, without ejecting your reader from the story. Many of us call it jarring or jolting. The last thing you want to do is jar a reader out of your story.

There are many ways you can inadvertently do this. Something as innocuous as a misspelled word can bring a reader to a complete stop to simply shake their head at the mistake or to reread the sentence to assure themselves of the meaning. You might get by with one misspelled word or awkward sentence in a chapter, but if you have two or more, the reader will likely become frustrated and might even stop reading altogether.

Many fiction writers like to create dialogue in a dialectic form to create authenticity, perhaps paying homage to a particular region of the country or their ancestors. While it can be effective to an extent, overdoing it can be very disruptive to the reader. While an author may consider it important, being forced to decipher thick dialect can be very frustrating and distracting to your reader.

Most readers have little patience for books that are hard to read, especially books that are intended to be for leisure. Even data-rich textbooks should be written in clear language.

Always remember to write from your reader's perspective. Put yourself in their reading chair, and write the story you would like to read. A good story, whether fiction or nonfiction, can also pull you along as the author.

But what about those times you can't think of what to write next? The dreaded writer's block.

What About Writer's Block

On the periphery of high-quality writing stands this thing called writer's block. It's a popular phrase among writers and even those who look upon the craft of writing from the outside. Writers decry this dreaded disease far too often.

The fact of the matter is it's a myth. As far as I know, there is no physical, physiological, or psychological abnormality called writer's block. As harsh as it may sound, the truth is, writer's block is an excuse and could well be renamed Distracted Writers Syndrome.

While not all writers are plotters, you should still have a good idea of what you are writing about. You should know the end or the culmination of the message you want to share, or the transformation you want for your readers. If you know you want to make points A, B, C, D, E, and F, but the words for point C aren't coming to you yet, skip over it, and move on to point D. Come back to C later.

If you need to step away from the manuscript, simply write in your journal and tell a short story about what happened to you yesterday. If you buy into the whole writer's block thing, you might just sit there frozen for days, giving yourself an excuse based on a false presumption of unconsciousness. It doesn't happen. No excuses.

What Kind of Writer Are You?

I've mentioned these a couple of times in passing. Author, Stephen King, in his book *On Writing*, identifies two types of writers—plotters and pantsers.

Plotters are those writers who take great pains to outline the entire book structure down to the chapter titles and section heading, knowing precisely what points will be made or scenes will be developed before the first word is written in the manuscript.

A pantser, on the other hand, is one who has an idea in mind and simply starts writing, counting on the completion of one scene or chapter to lead them to the next. Usually, a pantser at least has an ending in mind, but not necessarily. I think pantsers are most often associated with fiction writing.

Allow yourself the freedom to wander and experiment. As with anything, there is always danger in the extremes. If you are a diehard plotter and refuse to deviate from the outline, you stand the chance of missing unimagined opportunities and ending up with a lifeless manuscript. Who knows what pearls of wisdom you left on the table as you wrote past those stifled ideas?

On the other hand, a diehard pantser can be easily led down every rabbit hole that presents itself. Don't allow yourself to be deceived by your potentially less-than-focused characters.

Give every idea some thought, even in the middle of the writing process. If it adds to your message, grab on to it, and take it for the gift that it is. But if after thinking about it for a few minutes, you discover that it's leading you away from your message, jot it down somewhere so as not to lose it, then forget it, and carry on with your original thought. This is literally what is meant by setting something aside.

Types of Editing

When you and everyone else is finished cutting on your prose, have stopped sticking needles in it, and are no longer chopping up the story, it's time for one last pass before it goes to print—the final read-through.

To signal moving into this phase of the process, I like to print out the manuscript and put it in a binder. I even print out the book cover image and put it in the front cover sleeve of the binder to make it look somewhat professional.

Then, I find a quiet, out-of-the-way place (for me, it's the studio behind my house), take my binder along with one of my red Pilot Precise V5 pens, and I read through the manuscript one last time, marking any changes or corrections I need to make. The key here is reading it out loud to yourself. That's why I suggest getting away from everyone.

Once you've completed your final read-through and have incorporated the last batch of changes into your manuscript, it's time to execute the nerve-wracking step of submitting it to your editor.

Many writers are confused by the term *editing*. There are, indeed, several levels of editing, and they require separate and distinct skill sets from the editor. Once you've reached this phase of your book project, the train has left the station for some of these editors and it's too late to work with them on your current manuscript, so consider this ahead of time.

Ghostwriting

While ghostwriting isn't technically editing; it is an option available to the would-be author who may simply not have time to write a manuscript themselves. It is not unusual for a professional or an entrepreneur to not have the time or skill it takes to write a book. It simply isn't in their wheelhouse. Why would a veterinarian, for example, be expected to know how to write and publish a book simply because they need to as a business decision?

Enter the ghostwriter. A good ghostwriter is experienced and has had training in the art of getting inside that veterinarian's head to pull the story out. It happens through interviews, letters, journal notes, and emails. These days, it would also likely involve several Skype or Zoom chats.

The key to success is preserving the vet's own story and voice. It's a rather expensive option, but in the end, the vet has a book written with their name on it.

Ghostwriters typically include all aspects of the writing process in their packages and might include project management and publishing as well. The decision to include a ghostwriter's name on the cover or mention them on the copyright page is one made by you as the author and drastically lowers the cost.

Developmental Editing

At the top of the list of actual editing types is developmental editing. It falls short of ghostwriting because the author is performing the act of writing, but the editor provides a significant amount of help in setting up the book and developing the flow.

Here is a practical definition of developmental editing from the Reedsy website.

"A developmental edit is a thorough and in-depth edit of your entire manuscript. It is an examination of all the elements of your writing, from single words and the phrasing of individual sentences to overall structure and style. It can address plot holes or gaps, problematic characterization, and all other existing material.

"After a round of developmental editing—also called structural or substantive editing—a manuscript can change substantially; for inexperienced writers, accepting direct and honest feedback can be a difficult experience. Much of what you have spent many weeks, months, or even years writing can be cut, shaped, moved, or heavily criticized (positively).

"Good developmental editing will also consider your target audience and will judge your work in relation to professional industry standards and expectations. Only after your manuscript has been cut, reshaped, revised, and developed will it be ready for a copy edit and proofread." (Reedsy 2020)

I would venture to say that most authors don't use the services of a developmental editor as it is quite an expensive option. But if the highest quality product is the desired outcome, such as for a college-level textbook, or you are shopping the manuscript out through an agent to a potential publisher, it might be the way to go.

Line Editing

Line editing is not as in-depth for the editor as developmental editing but entails a little more than traditional copyediting. A line edit looks at the structure within and between paragraphs in each chapter to ensure words flow well. While a developmental editor might ensure the entire story flows from chapter to chapter and the message is consistent throughout, a line editor might perform the same function within a chapter. Often times, an author may hire an editor to perform two passes of the manuscript—a line edit followed by a copyedit.

Because I like to "treat the whole patient" when I edit, I will generally perform the line editing function as I copyedit a manuscript for my clients. This method won't be as thorough as a two-pass edit, but it saves the client a little time and money. It's a decision only you as the author can make based on the goals of your work.

Copyediting

When one thinks of editing a book, they normally think of spelling, punctuation, and grammar. This is the domain of a copyeditor. This is the deep look into the sentence structure and the words the author uses. Copyeditors notice when the author has used two spaces after a period and remove them.

Did you know that the use of two spaces after a sentence is old-school and is a holdover from the days of typewriters? Back in the day, typesetters needed to use the widest letter on the typewriter to determine a full space. That letter was "W" as it took up two spaces.

While a good copyeditor is never necessarily concerned about the proper English you learned in grade school, they do make sure your voice is clear and that style and usage is consistent. The standard style guide for typical trade publications—the fiction and nonfiction books you generally buy in a bookstore or download from Amazon—is *The Chicago Manual of Style*.

You may be familiar with the style guides you used in school, such as the APA (American Psychological Association guide). Some colleges use the Turabian Style Guide, which is the student version of *The Chicago Manual of Style*. Journalists use the *AP Style Guide* developed by the Associated Press.

It should be noted that authors break rules all the time, taking intentional creative license. Again, there is no expectation that you must write as though you are trying to pass an English grammar exam. On the contrary, originality and authenticity require something much different. While an experienced editor will generally look the other way when you deviate from a CMOS standard as long as it serves your book well, they will always call your attention to clarity and consistency issues. If it's a bump in the road for your reader, it must be addressed.

For example, if for some unknown reason, you refuse to use the Oxford/serial comma (the comma before the word *and* in a list), while you will break some hearts, I would likely give you a pass as long as you do it consistently throughout the manuscript. But if you write, "Kitchen, bedroom and living room" in one place and "Kitchen, bedroom, and living room" in another, I'm calling you out.

In a court case surrounding overtime laws, A federal appeals court in Maine ruled that the Oxford/serial comma must be used (but you still have the choice).

Six Dairy Drivers v. Oakhurst Dairy and Dairy Farmers of America, Inc. March 2017

Some things in CMOS are clearly stated as suggestions. Other items, such as how to cite references and quotations, use stronger language.

The bottom line is that you pay your editor to help you with clarity, consistency, and professionalism. You should always go to print with a high-quality product. Always. If you publish through Amazon KDP, they are not going to check your manuscript at all beyond making sure all of the text will fit in their template, and that's done by a machine, not a human. If you are an indie author, you own your mistakes.

There is one thing I always tell my editing clients: "Your book. Your story. Your voice." What I mean by that is this: any input an editor gives you is simply a recommendation. Editors typically use the Track Changes feature in MS Word to annotate your manuscript. This allows you, the author, to step through those recommendations and either accept or reject each one. The choice is completely yours. If you choose to stay with a misspelled word, ignoring the editor's recommendation (for reasons I cannot fathom), you can do that. There are no manuscript police . . . except your readers.

But in reality, you need to think long and hard before hitting that Reject button. Seriously. Is there a specific reason that you want to ignore that editor recommendation? Maybe there is. Most editors will ignore bad language in character dialogue since we know people don't speak perfect English. Colloquial or dialectic misspellings in dialogue should be kept to a minimum, and editors will know what you're doing and will usually overlook it. But if they edit it out and you want to keep it, that may be a good reason. You just have to remain aware of the potential consequences.

Some fiction authors go so overboard with this that it's often difficult to read. Your goal should always be ease of reading. You want to avoid jolting your reader out of the story with confusing language, or worse, mistakes. I don't know if it happens to you, but every time I run across a typo when reading a book, I pause to pass judgment. It jerks me out of the story. Then I have to reset and move on. As with most people, if it becomes so bad that the overall quality is in question, I no longer trust the author and set the book aside never to open it again. Unfair perhaps, but reality nonetheless.

You don't want that happening with your readers—even if your book is written just for family and friends . . . *especially* if your book is written for family and friends!

Proofreading

Consider hiring someone other than your editor for this task. By the time you reach this stage in the writing process, your editor, just like you, has become too close to the story to have the objective eye needed by a proofreader. Any good editor should recognize this and won't be bothered by your decision. Unless, of course, your editor can provide other people to do the proofreading, like mine does.

By this time, any changes to the manuscript should be minor, and a proofreader should keep their comments focused on blatant issues like typos that might distract the reader.

Again, this assumes that it has been professionally edited and only a few errors will be found. I've never had to do it, but if it becomes obvious that the book is still full of bad grammar and errors, and the change log method quickly becomes burdensome, it's probably a good indicator that the book should be sent back for another round of editing and the layout redone. The manuscript just isn't ready for primetime.

But again, I've never had to do this. Authors are usually self-conscious enough that they wouldn't allow it to happen. Most often, it's the other way around. I have to pry it out of their hands when their book comes up on my schedule for proofreading. I deal with a lot of perfectionism. Being a recovering perfectionist myself, I understand their reluctance to kick that bird out of the nest and let it fly.

"Done" beats "perfect" every time.

Research

Research is an important aspect of writing a book, whether fiction or non-fiction. You must always give credit where credit is due. You've heard it thousands of times throughout your life. When you decide to put things in writing, add a cover with your name on it, and publish it for public consumption, giving credit is doubly important. In fact, it's the law.

The Chicago Manual of Style has very specific instructions for citing the works of others and for how to quote people. Besides being a legal requirement, providing inline citations or endnotes always adds a look of professionalism to your work.

It's helpful to create a separate file to capture all of your sources. Don't forget to write down the source along with the details for citation as described by CMOS. Even websites and the specific web pages and articles should be cited.

Scrivener is one writing tool that contains the features necessary to save your research, even to the point of bringing in webpages and live links to the material you use.

Navigating research is a little less ominous for fiction writers. They are generally researching locations and perhaps some historical figures, but there isn't much of a reason to cite sources. But the copyright laws still apply. Name your sources if you use them verbatim.

You are working hard to become a successful author. Do what is right. Cite your sources.

Cover Quality

As I mentioned earlier, whether standing in front of bookshelves at Barnes and Noble or perusing through the best sellers on Amazon, the first thing that gets your attention is the book cover. The colors, the fonts, the images all come together to reach out and slap you. Only then do you look at the title.

Of course, there are those times when you're looking for a specific A-List author, but I venture to say that often, you have no idea who the author is, nor do you really care. The cover has captured your interest, first the front, then the title, then the blurb on back. It's a predictable sequence of events for any book shopper.

The worst thing you could do as an author is skimp on the quality of your cover. Unless you are a skilled graphic designer, familiar with the intricacies of book cover design and the associated genre markets, never attempt to do this at home. It's a risky business. Many authors even change their covers after a period of time when nothing is happening, and they determine the cover is clearly not garnering the attention it should.

It may be the best story in the world lying between those covers, but nobody will ever know because the cover is easily ignored.

In this age of online shopping, the term *thumbnail* has become a well-known term in the industry. Your book cover must look good as a thumbnail.

So, what does that mean? Look through the book cover images on Amazon. Notice how small they are on your computer screen when they are listed side by side. Notice how small the covers are on the screen of your phone. Pretty tiny, right?

The important thing is that you can still see the basic premise of the image and can clearly read the title. The name of the author may be too small to make out on many of these covers, but the author isn't that important unless it's one worthy of having their name bigger than the title itself. There's a reason for that. Many readers do look for authors, not titles. When you attain this status enjoyed by the likes of Tom Clancy, James Patterson, Danielle Steel, John Grisham, or J. K. Rowling, maybe it's time to make your name bigger than the title too.

There are two critical elements in modern day book covers: a clearly visible title (no flourished fonts cluttering the landscape), and an image that easily reflects the genre of the book. The most beautifully designed book cover in the world means nothing unless it can capture your reader's attention at the size of a postage stamp.

Get a professionally designed book cover.

6.

HUMAN RESOURCES MANAGEMENT

What is Human Resources Management?

Of course, we're all probably somewhat familiar with what HR is. But, what in the world does HR have to do with writing a book? Glad you asked! Human Resources Management is typically the skills and abilities associated with hiring and nurturing the human aspect of a project—your people.

The project manager, the author (you in this case), has the responsibility for gathering the people necessary to get the job done and to ensure they become valued stakeholders and are kept in the loop regarding all things that pertain to your book.

My people? What people? I'm referring to those people we've just been talking about—your cover designer, editor, interior layout designer, copywriter, etc.

While these team members are likely to be independent contractors—not employed by you directly—you still owe them the courtesy of providing them the information they need, when they need it, and keeping them abreast of the status of the overall project. They are stakeholders in your project.

For example, the interior layout designer is waiting for your finished manuscript so they can get to work on setting it up for print. You've undoubtedly agreed to a date and put it on the calendar, so everyone knows when to expect this delivery. You have to communicate between your editor and your layout designer, so everyone knows what's happening.

Unlike a normal HR department, you aren't responsible for the training, safety, and security of these team members, but you do need to ensure they have what they need to help you complete your project.

If you are conducting your writing practice as a business, you may have to concern yourself with things like ensuring you have an IRS W9 form on file for each member of the team providing services in excess of a set value, currently $600. Of course, you should always consult your accountant or tax expert for the latest information. It's also worth knowing that if you pay your vendors via PayPal, the IRS considers this to be adequate documentation and a W9 isn't required. But again, follow your accountant's instructions. By the way, your bookkeeper or accountant is also a member of your team, so treat them accordingly.

These are all considerations for you not only as a project manager, but also as a business owner, even if there is no intention to make this a business book. There are several great resources available for this specific purpose. One I highly recommend is actually a very tiny book called *Business and Tax Tips for Writers* by Carol Topp, CPA—available through my website at TerryStafford.com/resources/pmw.

Your Writing Team

Below is a list of your typical team members and what each will need from you as project manager and Human Resources overseer.

Cover Designer

Your book cover designer is critical to the team. You will need to share not only the genre of the book but also the story itself and the message you are wanting to convey. Often, the cover designer will attempt to capture a scene or a key character from the book if it's fiction. If it's nonfiction, the designer must understand the concepts you are teaching or perhaps the most important point of the book.

In some cases, you may have to bare your soul so the designer can capture your heart for the readers. None of this is meant to imply that your cover will be a complex mix of all of these things. An experienced cover designer will know how to boil all of these complex ideas down into a simple design while carefully using imagery and fonts appropriate for your genre and market.

One aspect of cover design that will have to wait until after the interior layout designer is complete is the spine's thickness. To calculate that, the final page count and selected paper color are required.

The cover designer will also need the logo file for your publisher imprint for the back cover and spine as well as the ISBN for the back cover. Designers can usually create the necessary barcode to go along with the ISBN. If needed, Bowker will provide an option to purchase and download the associated barcode image.

There are specific file image requirements for different distribution platforms and book formats. The cover file delivered for an eBook will be different from that provided for a paperback book on Amazon KDP. There is also a different file needed if you are publishing a hardcover book through Ingram Spark, and yet another file if you are publishing for Kindle and another for Apple Books. Your designer should be familiar with all of these requirements and will provide all the files you need. Many designers will also provide cover images suitable for marketing and promotions on social media.

Editor

Once an agreement has been signed with your chosen editor, often after a deposit is paid, the editor will place you on their calendar. When the agreed-to date approaches, they are waiting for you. You should make every attempt to ensure that your manuscript is delivered to them on time. If you know you aren't going to make it, communicate early and often with them so they can plan accordingly. As I write this, I have three editing clients who have all slipped their dates a few times each. It's doable but can result in a considerable amount of juggling to make everyone happy.

It forces me into a first-come-first-served shootout. If I get two or all three at the same time, someone will have to wait, and I'm guessing they will become antsy and frustrated. Don't let this happen to you. Plan carefully as we discussed in the Time Management chapter, and deliver on time.

Know that you are finished. After going through a couple of editing passes yourself, you should be comfortable with what you have written. Do not expect to be able to send your manuscript a chapter or section at a time. It's never a good idea, and most experienced editors would never accept it that way.

Unless an editor is prone to sending status updates, you may not hear from them for a couple weeks while they are editing. Unless the wait is excessive, don't pester them. I like to punch out an email to the client when I'm about halfway through the manuscript just to let them know I'm working on it. The next time they hear from me will be the delivery of the completed edit unless I have a question.

Of course, if your relationship with the editor also includes coaching or consulting, which I also provide if requested, the communication will be much different. In that case, I'm usually speaking with the author at least three times per month while the manuscript is being written. So, when it comes time to edit, I'm already familiar with the story, and there may be question-and-answer periods throughout the editing process. But again, don't expect that much communication with a normal author–editor relationship.

Interior Layout Designer

Once your edit is complete and you have incorporated all of the recommended changes, you should read through the manuscript again to ensure that everything is the way you want it to go to a proofreader and to print. It's a crucial time since things are about to become permanent.

Having said that, we go back to the idea that *done* is better than *perfect*. The beauty of being an indie author is that making changes to an already published work isn't that hard. It happens all the time. So, don't allow yourself to become paralyzed here. But know that it's a critical step.

When you're ready, submit the manuscript to your interior layout designer. They will often provide you with an intake form on their website where you can decide on the template you want to use, the type of paper you will be printing on, any specifications you want to provide, such as the clipart used for scene breaks in novels or the files you want to upload for infographics throughout the book. Make sure your cover designer has provided you with black and white cover images for the title page and half-title page. Your layout person will need those.

If your requests are more complicated, or you don't trust your ability to explain them clearly in writing, don't hesitate to request a phone call with the designer.

You will also need to specify the file types you need based on your distribution channels. You should generally receive ePub, PDF, and mobi files. I also like to request .docx and the InDesign file set in case I want to make some minor changes myself. Some companies may consider those to be proprietary, but it won't hurt to ask. If it's important to you, ask providers if they will provide you with the InDesign files, and choose not to work with the ones who will not.

If there are any significant changes you want to make later, perhaps a new edition, the designer should have your book on file and available to incorporate your changes.

When your interior designer is finished, you need to get the page count back to your cover designer so they can complete the spine dimensions. I mentioned the paper color earlier. Typically, nonfiction books are printed on white paper while novels are printed on what is known in the industry as cream-colored paper. Of course, you can choose whatever you want, but just know that cream is thicker than white, which is why the cover designer needs to know the page count and the color to calculate the width of the spine of the book.

Proofreader

Proofreading comes just before uploading your book for publication. Because of this, as a proofreader, I like to see the book in its final form after the layout is complete and in PDF format. My designer always provides me with the PDF along with a .docx log file to list the errors and their locations. I can point out how it currently reads and how I want it to read. For this reason alone, there shouldn't be many changes to make, and they should all be minor. It's not a time to continue the editing process.

Some proofreaders want the MS Word file of the manuscript to continue to use the Track Changes function before it goes to interior layout. If that's what your proofreader wants, then so be it. But I think it invites a perpetual editing loop if not a fear of letting it go.

Copywriter

A copywriter, not to be confused with copyrighting, is the wordsmith you employ to create the sales copy on the back cover of your book. You may also hire them to write other related marketing material later on, but for our purposes here, you need to focus on the back cover.

The copywriter will need to know how many words they can use. That should be coordinated with the cover designer to ensure all of the back-cover elements are considered. The elements that you and your designer must consider are the back-cover copy, tag lines, endorsements, author image and bio, ISBN, barcode, and anything else you choose to put there.

Not all of these elements are used on all books. That's why decisions must be made for which ones to use and the sizes available within the real estate for each. For example, I have chosen to keep my author photo and bio off of the back cover and place it in the back matter of the book instead. That leaves more room for text on the back.

You can also choose to use less text in a larger font size. If your blurb has too many words with small fonts, it may discourage people from reading it. Often, the verbiage for the blurb is provided, and the cover designer fits it in at the largest available font. If it's too small, then you have to go back and ask the copywriter to use fewer words. You could also decide to eliminate other elements like tag lines or endorsements.

The point is that these elements must all be coordinated by you, the project manager. Of course, you can always get out of the middle and ask your copywriter to call your cover designer directly and let you know what they come up with—your choice as the project manager.

You may have other team members helping you with your book. Always be aware that the actions of one member may impact the actions of another. Communication between all members is essential to a happy team and a professionally published book.

7.

COMMUNICATIONS MANAGEMENT

What is Communications Management?

Communications Management is simply the act of ensuring that all stakeholders on the project remain abreast of what's happening. For writers, that generally means emailing your team on a regular basis, so everyone is aware of any schedule slips or changes in strategy. If you are an entrepreneur, you are well aware that busy people don't like surprises.

Perhaps you have asked your cover designer to begin creating the cover for your book early, but then you change the entire premise of the story that renders the direction you gave them inappropriate. That's the risk of early design I was referring to in previous chapters. Don't wait to let them know a new design is necessary. It gives them the opportunity to at least stop working on what they're doing for you. Expect to pay for the changes and possibly take a hit on the schedule.

If you are already a published author with a reader following, another aspect of Communications Management might be keeping your readers abreast of your writing through newsletters or social media posts. Devoted fans are definitely stakeholders in this regard and will love to hear about your journey as an author. Don't disappoint.

You will undoubtedly recruit your Advanced Reader Team, or ART, from your reader email subscribers list. If you intend to publish the book you are writing, your ART will be a tremendous help leading up to your launch day by sharing your book promotions with their friends and providing you with those all-important book reviews.

Keeping Everyone Informed

Creating a complete and comprehensive communications plan isn't necessary as an author, but simply be aware of your team and know that they are relying on you to keep them abreast of your progress. Know what each member needs to know and when they need to know it.

For example, just because I like to have my covers done early doesn't mean that the cover is complete. It's only designed to the point that I have an image of the front.

The back cover and the spine are still pending at that point. You have four stakeholders involved in this step who are depending on you for communications—yourself, your cover designer, your copywriter, and your interior layout designer.

Your cover designer needs to be kept apprised of the status of the back-cover copy from your copywriter, the final page count from your layout designer, and the paper color from you. As I mentioned earlier, the spine width cannot be determined without the page count and paper color.

So, you see why clear communication is important to this process. Help your team help you by keeping them in the loop.

What Does It Look Like?

Another area where communication is critical is with your editor and layout designer. If your layout designer has you on their calendar, and you are late getting your manuscript to your editor, everybody needs to know. If you are two weeks late to your editor, does that mean the layout designer needs to find an open slot for you two weeks later on their calendar?

Not necessarily. Close communication with your editor may reveal that they can move a little faster and can have your manuscript ready in only one week. Don't expect this, but it never hurts to ask.

In that case, you are delivering the file to your layout designer only a week late. If the stars are aligned·and you're lucky, if your layout designer can get his work done in one week instead of two, your book is still on schedule. Again, not everyone has that kind of leeway in their schedule, but it never hurts to ask. If your team bends over backward like this to help you stay on schedule, you need to pile on the praise and email plenty of gift cards for free coffee.

Keeping your book on schedule through the ebb and flow of the writing process is your job as the project manager and requires plenty of communication. Make no assumptions, and go overboard with clarity.

It's one thing to communicate a message; it's quite another for that message to be received and clearly understood. If one of the tasks you are tracking is on the critical path and you shoot a text out to your layout designer that it could be a couple days late, is your project management responsibility fulfilled?

No, it is not. How many times have you sent a text to a spouse or friend asking them to stop and pick up a loaf of bread only to have them arrive empty handed?

"Didn't you get my text?"

"No, I didn't see it," they say, looking down at their phone. "Oh, there it is!"

Don't relegate your book to unanswered texts. If they don't respond in a reasonable amount of time, make the effort to punch the numbers in and call them.

Same thing with email. Many people these days don't have time to continually check their email. If something is time sensitive, pick up the phone and call. I know it's old fashioned, but it can also save your bacon.

The same can be said regarding all of your stakeholders. Just because you once mentioned in a newsletter to your readers that you have a new book coming out, don't assume they saw it. When you launch and they didn't know about it, they could be genuinely upset. Mention the book in more than one newsletter and on more than one social media channel. Promoting is communicating.

As a consummate introvert myself, I have to work on this communication thing persistently. It's not something that comes easy to me. But . . .

You are the project manager. Communicate.

Friends and Influencers

As I said, promoting is communicating. Your book can't get into the people's hands if they don't know about it. This is the realm of marketing.

I've made it perfectly clear that this book is not about marketing because that is something I continue to learn myself. But if you put marketing and promoting into its simplest terms, it is communicating. Your readers are stakeholders. Therefore, your potential readers are potential stakeholders.

Bestselling author Honorée Corder, famous for her work on the Miracle Morning series with Hal Elrod, among many other things, is an expert in the marketing arena. One of her signature moves in marketing is giving her books away profusely.

While many gurus will tell you that the tactic is a quick way to the poor house, she sees it as promotion. She communicates on her platform about her books via the books themselves. She even goes so far as randomly leaving her books in coffee shops and waiting rooms. What a better way to communicate your book than having your book cover lying all over the place.

But how will you make money if you give them the book? You don't. Not from *that* book, anyway. But you might make somebody a reader—a stakeholder. If you're really lucky, that random reader becomes a raving fan. If they rave about your book to ten of their friends, you could have another ten stakeholders wanting to get on your email list to receive your newsletter. As Honorée says, it's about the long game.

It's also worth saying that you don't have to communicate alone. You have friends (perhaps known and unknown) that you can rely on to help you communicate to those potential stakeholders. You might even know some influencers. Remember when I said you need to get to know other authors? You need to get to know a bunch of 'em! Make friends with them.

You never want to use or abuse your friends, but your author friends especially will want to help you. Some of them may have a huge following themselves or will likely know influencers that are willing to help. The secret is, find out who the influencers are, get to know them by getting familiar with their work, and help them.

That's right. Find a way to help influencers. Be a servant. If they help you in return, fine. If they don't, fine. At least you may have made a new friend. Friends can be stakeholders in your work as well. Of course, you aren't going to go around referring to them that way.

"Hi. I'd like you to meet my stakeholder, James Patterson." Yeah, don't do that.

But you get what I mean.

8.

RISK MANAGEMENT

What is Risk Management?

Simply put, Risk Management is the art and science of knowing exactly what to do when something goes wrong. At NASA, this requires teams of people following every step of the planning process. Rigorous risk-mitigation plans are developed for each phase and at each location.

At each step along the development path, engineers analyze what could go wrong, what the likelihood is that it will go wrong, what the impact to the process is if it does go wrong, and the specific action that will be taken if it goes wrong. This is all plugged into elaborate mathematical formulas resulting in a bevy of charts and graphs that line the walls of conference rooms around the country.

In formal Risk Management, there are only a few responses to consider at the 40,000-foot level.

1. **Avoid the risk:** Change your strategy or plans. For writers, this might be deciding not to write a book at all. Don't do that. Some risk avoidance is healthy. Excessive risk avoidance is

an invitation to avoid living altogether. If an interview falls through on one of your chapters, perhaps you decide to delete that chapter.

2. **Mitigate the risk:** Take action to reduce the risk. For example, develop work procedures and equipment designed to reduce workplace safety risks. For writers, this might mean becoming an expert at managing your schedule.

3. **Transfer the risk:** Defer the risk to a third party like an insurance company. Not much you can do here as a writer except turn it over to a ghostwriter. It's an expensive proposition, but people do it all the time. You want a book but want to transfer the headache? Get a ghostwriter.

4. **Accept the risk:** Decide to just jump in and take the risk. This is . . . well . . . risky. But some things just aren't worth fretting over. If it happens, it happens. Que será será. This is appropriate for things that just aren't that likely to happen anyway, or if they do, it won't cause much harm—like spilt milk on that chapter you printed out this morning and spread across the dining table.

As with the communications plan, you won't need to be familiar with these formal responses or develop a full-on Risk Management plan. But if you are going to publish your book and you have set a launch date that all of your stakeholders are interested in, it will probably behoove you to at least think through the process, beginning to end, and think about what could go wrong.

When Something Goes Wrong

The amount of effort you put into the assessment of each risk is proportional to the odds of it happening. For example, if you plan on publishing to the Amazon KDP platform, as most indie authors do, you might assess what to do if Amazon all the sudden goes out of business. It could happen, but the odds are extremely low—at least for the foreseeable future. So, you wouldn't want to put in a lot of time fretting over it and developing mitigation plans.

You might just think to yourself, *If Amazon stops publishing books, I'll just jump over to Apple Books or Ingram Spark.* Maybe even look at each of their author services websites to become loosely familiar with their process. Okay . . . next!

On the other hand, what happens if two months after you sign an agreement with a book cover designer, they decide they can't or don't want to provide that service anymore? Of course, you could rush around and try to find another designer who can fit you in on short notice, or you can take a few minutes during your project planning to create a list of two or three backup designers who have been recommended to you by people you trust. Then, if it happens, you're prepared.

Again, you want to keep that planning effort proportional to the odds of it happening, so don't get wrapped around the axle on it. As you look at your schedule, pay particular attention to the points of handoff.

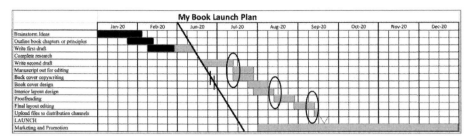

Figure 4 Potential Problem Areas

If something is going to go wrong, it will usually happen as the result of someone being late to the transition from one phase of the project to the next.

Here are some ideas for you to consider during your risk assessment. Again, don't get too worried about this, but it's worth a quick consideration.

Risk:

1. I can't make the agreed-to delivery date for my manuscript to the editor.
    a. Mitigation: (How do I prevent it from happening?)
        i. Ensure that I meet all subtask commitments on my calendar.
        ii. Maintain constant contact with the editor, especially during the weeks ahead of delivery.
    b. Response: (What do I do if it happens?)
        i. Discuss options with the editor early on. Arrange a secondary delivery date?

2. Amazon can't get the files up on my sales page in time for my launch date. (It happens.)
   a. Mitigation:
      i. Plan my uploads to occur at least a week ahead of launch.
      ii. Coordinate the early upload with my interior layout designer and proofreader. Have all files in hand fifteen days before launch.
   c. Response:
      i. Call Amazon and speak to a human being to assess the situation.
      ii. Communicate with your stakeholders. (Readers, influencers, marketers, etc.)

Here are a few other areas you may want to look at regarding risk assessment:

- What happens if you can't maintain the writing pace you planned on?
- What happens if you can't deliver your manuscript on time?
- What happens if your editor takes longer than agreed to?
- What happens if your editor returns your manuscript still full of errors?
- What happens if your cover designer just can't get your vision right?
- What happens if your copywriter, God forbid, has a heart attack?
- What happens if an unexpected life event causes you to pause your writing and launch plans?

- What happens if your proofreader strongly recommends that you return to the editing phase?
- What happens if your computer crashes? Hint: make lots of backups in the cloud.

As you can see, there are many things that *could* go wrong. Just a quick analysis of the timeline, handoffs, and technology, along with jotting down a few notes during planning could save you a lot of stress and lost time later on. The point of this short chapter is merely to encourage you to give Risk Management some thought, not to paralyze you.

9.

PROCUREMENT MANAGEMENT

What is Procurement Management?

At NASA, Procurement Management is essentially contract management—how they get the products and services they need to get things done. Likewise, for writers, it is simply the act of getting the products and services you need. It's closely related to Cost Management but is primarily focused on the administration of the writing business.

Of course, getting the products and tools you need is accomplished as any normal purchase; from a computer store, an online resource like Amazon, an office supply store, etc.

But getting services nailed down is another story altogether. Because services are not a physical product you can hold in your hand or a computer program you can open and plainly see in operation, they are more difficult to verify. How do you know you are getting what you paid for?

Getting What You Need

The service industry typically does business with proposals and agreements. They come in many different sizes and shapes. Some service providers may be okay with a verbal agreement over the phone, but I highly recommend against it, especially when money is changing hands.

The complexity of any agreement is generally proportional to the size of the task to be done. I recently asked my book cover designer to compile a cover for the release of a digital box set for a trilogy I just completed.

He already had the covers on file, so it was a small task for him. I asked for the cover via email, he quoted a price in his email response, and I approved it, again, via email. I had the digital cover in my inbox the following day. It was that simple. It wouldn't have made sense for him to send me a five-page agreement for a job that simple. The associated risk was very small.

On the other hand, a ghostwriter agreement can be many pages long. Ghostwriting entails a relationship over many months, if not years. It usually involves a lot of money and many data-collection meetings. A lot can go wrong in a ghostwriting relationship if not well coordinated and properly managed with very specific goals and agreements. In other words, the risk to both the author and the ghostwriter is high.

When I am approached by an author to take advantage of my editing services, I get the working title, estimated word count, and a sample chapter from them if available. I use the first two data points to develop a proposal using my standard template where I list my price for the service and what the agreement would look like. I submit that along with a sample edit of the chapter they provided for their review and consideration.

If they like what they see and want to enter into a contract (normally confirmed with a simple email notification), I simply change the title of the proposal to say Agreement, confirm all of the dates, and email a PDF document to them for electronic signature. I use SignNow, but there are many electronic signature services available. DocuSign is another popular company that comes to mind.

I'll provide a copy of my Proposal/Agreement Template in the resources section in the back of this book. I only provide it as an example of what you might see from your service providers. As the author, you don't have to come up with these agreements. They will be specific to each of your team members.

Many of the vendors you work with as an author require a considerable amount of information to serve you. Some have an online intake form to collect everything. For example, a cover designer will need to know things like the genre of the book, the message and feel you want to portray, the finished size of the book, page count, paper color, back-cover copy, etc.

They may also need you to select a service level. For example, some book cover designers will provide a number of marketing images in their packages and in varying formats and sizes that you can select up front.

In this cover designer example, you may not have all of the information up front, especially if you have your cover designed early like I do. You won't have the page count until after your interior layout designer has finished the layout. From that, you can see the page count to relay that information to your cover designer.

Your interior layout designer will have intake requirements as well. You will likely need to select a template for them to set up. They will usually have many styles to choose from that will be categorized as either fiction or nonfiction. There is a psychology involved with these designs, so it's best to go with what the professionals recommend, at least within the groupings they provide.

Unless you are a trained designer, requesting a custom setup can be risky. If a potential reader picks up your novel, and it has the look and feel of a textbook, they will likely put it back on the shelf, literally or figuratively.

Where to Find Your Team

If this is your first rodeo, pulling a team together can be a daunting task. While there are many websites you can visit (and many are very impressive), the best source available, by far, is referrals from experienced authors. That's why it is so important to garner as many relationships as you can with other authors. The wealth of experience they have and help they can provide is priceless.

It's easy to find and join some good quality Facebook groups for writers. There are also writer's groups on LinkedIn and Pinterest. Check them out, and make connections early, preferably with those who write in the same genre as you. Find out who they know, like, and trust to do their design work and editing.

Once you've established relationships with these service providers yourself, you will likely return to them over and over again unless they give you a good reason not to. Don't be surprised if they become good friends and supporters of your work. Then you become a resource for other up-and-coming authors.

You can find good designers and editors on services like Fiverr and Upwork, but be extremely careful and selective if you choose to go that route. Many of the freelancers on these services are overseas. Don't get me wrong; there are excellent designers all over the world. It's worth repeating. Check out Jennifer Harshman's book, *Find a Real Editor.* Many parts of it can apply to all services providers.

But consider the risk. I would be hesitant to hire an editor who lives outside the country. I would be suspect of their American English experience. Of course, there are many Americans who live overseas and do this work, so nothing is absolute. Just know who you are working with.

I hired a book cover designer on Fiverr for my first novel through their bid process. I posted some pictures I had taken and asked the bidders to incorporate one of them into a cover design. I got some great proposals with beautiful covers. I think only one of about fifteen bidders was actually from the US.

I selected the cover that I loved and began working with that designer. The communications were a bit rocky across the language barrier, but it went well. Then, after the book was published, that designer became very unresponsive to requests for follow-up work. I needed to have the back-cover copy changed. He agreed to do the work in one note but then wouldn't respond after that. He fell off the edge of the earth. I hope he is in good health, but it was very frustrating.

I ended up having to go to a designer here in the states who was able to reverse engineer the original cover graphics and recreate it with the new back-cover copy. It was a pain that could have been avoided with the right choice to begin with. It's hard to have regrets because the cover is just so darn gorgeous. But still, it would have been much more productive if I could have kept a good working relationship with the original designer.

Therein lies the problem. It was obvious to me that it was simply a transaction with the overseas designer when I was looking for a relationship. Know the difference, and act accordingly. Just be careful.

Where Not to Find Your Team

I only include this section because I've heard horror stories from would-be authors who were traumatized by their experience with these people. We've all heard that doing business with family or friends can be the ruin of both. There are obviously a bajillion successful family businesses out there, so there's nothing absolute about this. But here are a few points to ponder.

- Just because your sister is a high school English teacher doesn't mean she knows how to edit a romance novel.
- Just because your friend next door can create a great brochure for neighborhood events doesn't mean he can design a cover for a book on leadership.
- Just because your mom is your biggest fan and simply wants to help doesn't make her a good choice to be your proofreader.

Again, these are not off limits if they really are professionals in the book industry. We should be so lucky as to have those kinds of friends. But choose wisely. If you have friends and family who simply want to help, they would probably be great candidates to add to your list of beta readers or even your ART, but not your technical team.

Distribution Considerations

Another aspect of the business, if you are planning to become a published author, is book distribution. The obvious choice for indie authors is Amazon KDP. But there are many others to choose from.

Ingram Spark is another great choice for on-demand printing and distribution. If you plan to print a hardcover edition of your book, they may be the only game in town, at least in the indie space.

When you upload your files to Amazon KDP, you will need to select your expanded distribution channels. This gets you into international markets. If you're going to also distribute with Ingram Spark, you may choose to forgo expanded distribution with Amazon and instead, opt for Ingram's catalog, which is used by retailers and libraries around the globe.

If you sign up for Amazon's KDP Select, it will get you into their Kindle Unlimited library and some of the promotional services they provide. However, signing up for KDP Select locks you in for ninety days at a time and requires that you sell your ebook (Kindle) exclusively through Amazon channels. Many new authors choose to start off exclusive to Amazon, and once they have a following, they switch over to go wide.

Wide is the term used when you opt to use as many distribution channels as you or your team can handle. There are many companies in the industry whose purpose is simply to take your book and distribute it wide for you. Consider companies like Kobo and Draft2Digital. There are many others in that space, so shop around and get referrals from your author friends.

10.

STAKEHOLDER MANAGEMENT

Much of what we've already discussed falls under Stakeholder Management. It's an important step to take time and consciously determine who your stakeholders are and how you will interact with them. Stakeholder Management is closely related to Communications Management in that you must communicate with your stakeholders, or you will lose them.

Here is a list of stakeholders that most writers will need to consider in the order (loosely) that you will need to consider them, though not all are required:

- Beta readers
- Editor/Coach
- Interior layout designer
- Book cover designer
- Advance Reader Team
- Copywriter
- Publisher/Distributors
- Influencers
- Readers
- Marketers

These days, you will find that most interaction with the members of your tech team will be via email. But always consider the message to be conveyed and the clarity required when deciding your method of interaction.

If a sentence will do, a text message is probably fine. If a simple idea must be shared that will require more than a sentence, email is a good choice. For complex conversations that may require back-and-forth iterations, pick up the phone.

It's good practice to recognize how many times an email goes back and forth. If you're on the third reply of one of your email threads, it might be time to make a phone call.

Again, the key element in communicating with these stakeholders is clarity. The more you communicate, the less likely there will be problems to overcome. Consider it risk mitigation.

With stakeholders who are readers, your communication will likely be one-way, but it doesn't have to be. If you send a newsletter to your email list of readers, and someone responds, it's almost always via email. Answer them! Start up a conversation. That's the way to turn readers into raving fans.

There are other ways to communicate with these stakeholders like podcasts, a YouTube channel, blog posts, etc. Always be attentive to reader responses. Make them feel important (which they are), and you will have a fan for life.

Stakeholder Expectations

Another aspect of Stakeholder Management is managing expectations. The reason you have gone through the trouble of identifying stakeholders is because you, as the project manager, must ensure that your stakeholders are happy. No, better than happy—elated.

The best way to make sure they are happy is by making sure you meet or exceed their expectations. So, what does that mean? It means putting yourself in their shoes.

If you were an editor, what would you expect from an author client? On-time manuscript delivery? Excellent communications?

What about your readers? What will they expect? A high-quality, attention-grabbing book cover? A professionally written story?

Every one of your stakeholders has an interest in your book. That's why you have identified them as a stakeholder. It stands to reason that if they have an interest or a stake in your book, there are expectations attached to it.

If you are planning to be traditionally published, one of your stakeholders is the publishing house. When they signed you on, they did so with the expectation that you will make them money. If you were lucky enough to be paid an advance, the publishing house expects for your book to make at least that amount in sales and hopefully a profit for everyone on top of that.

In that case, a publishing house becomes a highly invested stakeholder with grandiose expectations. That's why publishing with a traditional publisher can get so complicated and burdensome.

What are some of the other expectations of your stakeholders? We mentioned it earlier: your cover designer expects to get the page count and paper color from you in order to complete your book cover design. The expectation (and likely the contract agreement) is that you will provide that information before they can deliver your cover.

Never forget who your stakeholders are and what they want or need.

11.

LESSONS LEARNED

What Is/Are Lessons Learned?

Lessons Learned is a concept that comes under varying headings. The military might call it an After-Action Report. Some project managers refer to it as a Postmortem Report. At NASA, we just called it Lessons Learned and maintained them in a Lessons Learned database.

So, what is it? It's exactly what the name suggests. These are the lessons you learn along the way while managing a project. If you plan to write and publish more than one book, and I certainly hope you do, you don't want to find yourself making the same mistakes over and over. By the way, you *will* make mistakes.

As you proceed through all of these wickets we've been discussing throughout this book, it's a good idea to keep a document on hand specifically for Lessons Learned. It might be a paper notebook, it might be Word document, or it might be a spreadsheet. If you really want to geek out, you can create a database using something like Microsoft Access or SQL. But that's getting way serious. Maybe if (when) you get to be as busy as James Patterson with a whole team of writers, that will make sense.

The point is, each time you learn something important as you navigate the writing process, it's a good idea to capture it so you can either avoid it or take advantage of it next time around. Even if you fail to write things down as you go, once the project is finished, you should still sit quietly and reflect on the things you learned.

Capture those aha! moments or those things you don't want to ever have to go through again. After you've captured them, you can review them when it's time to start the next project. You might even want to take one of them a step further and modify your documented system to incorporate the lesson learned.

Then What?

When you begin your next book project and are in the process of developing your book proposal, review your Lessons Learned, and plan how you will take advantage of them or avoid them.

Lessons learned are not always a bad thing. Many of them are things you learned along the way that might be exciting new discoveries or simpler ways of doing things.

Perhaps you discovered a new tool that makes your life easier. Include that in your workflow on the next go around. And don't forget to keep your Lessons Learned going through each iteration of your writing practice. You'll still be learning new things on your fourth and fifth books.

Never open a new book project again feeling like you're a total beginner. Now you have the tools you need to be a prolific writer in the
most efficient way possible. You have repeatable systems.

12.

NEXT STEPS

Where to Go from Here

Now that you have your writing systems in place, what are you doing with writing? If you intend to publish your books to sell on Amazon KDP or Ingram Spark or one of the many other distributors, you'll need to learn how to market your book.

These days, that doesn't mean salesy pitches to your friends and family. It means building relationships with people who want to help you and people who enjoy your work. Again, I didn't go into book marketing because I'm just not an expert in that aspect of the publishing industry. But I'm working on it! Maybe I'll include in the 2nd edition.

Perhaps you're writing a blog or other website content. You should now have plenty of ideas for keeping your work organized. Many of the same principles apply. People can't appreciate your work if they don't know it exists. Building relationships through social media and email lists is a critical component of making people aware.

One thing to always keep in mind as you go forward is that you own your email list. Social media outlets can disappear overnight, taking your friends and contacts with them. Remember Myspace? Well, maybe you don't. Many people, especially musicians, relied on Myspace to communicate with their followers. It still exists, almost exclusively for musicians now, but I don't know anyone who actually uses it or consumes content there. It has simply faded away.

The bottom line is that you should share content and build relationships. If you haven't already, start an email list using one of the email service providers like MailChimp, MailerLite, ConvertKit, Aweber, etc.

We All Need Help

Writing a book or consistent social posts isn't an easy endeavor. But it does become much easier when you get your systems in place and at least feel organized. If you need help, search it out. There are many writing consultants and coaches available who can help you set up systems. There are many communities online that exist for the sole purpose of helping each other.

If you want one-on-one attention with me, feel free to reach out. I'll be glad to set up a call with you to see how I might be able to help. You can email me at terry@terrystafford.com.

I look forward to hearing from you. Good luck with your writing, and I hope to see your message out in the world someday soon.

Sláinte

13.

RESOURCES

Book Proposal Template

Here is a list of questions to answer as you gather data for your book proposal. You can choose to format it as an outline like I did in chapter one, or just leave it as a basic Q&A list for now. You can get that template at terrystafford.com/resources/pmw if you want to use it. But the important thing is the data. If you choose to seek out an agent to help you get into the hands of a traditional publisher, you will certainly need to formalize this.

Agents often have a template they want you to follow, and even publishers may have an online form for you to gather this information. The important thing is having it all on hand. You need it whether you choose to publish or not just to gather your thoughts.

BOOK PROPOSAL STRUCTURE

Title Page

I. The Content

  A. Premise

  B. Unique Selling Proposition

  C. Overview

  D. Manuscript

    1. Manuscript Status

    2. Special Features

    3. Anticipated Manuscript Length

    4. Anticipated Manuscript Completion Date

II. The Market

  A. Demographic Description

  B. Psychographic Description

  C. Affinity Groups

  D. Competition

III. The Author

  A. Background

  B. Previous Writing

  C. Personal Marketing

Chapter-by-Chapter Synopsis

Sample Chapters

Service Proposal/Agreement

Here is a copy of the Proposal/Agreement that I use for my editing clients. This is provided only as an example of what you may get from the team members you choose to provide the necessary services. I change the title from work-for-hire Proposal to work-for-hire Agreement once the client agrees with everything. Then I finalize it with dates and send it back in a pdf for electronic signature via SignNow. Again, this is but one way your service provider can gain your commitment. Some may use something as simple as an email message and response to close the deal.

LOGO

Cover Page

Enclosed is a work-for-hire Proposal

submitted by

Terry Stafford

to provide editing services for

Client Name

and the work entitled

Book Title

When completed and signed, this proposal becomes a binding agreement between the editor and the author and can only be modified with a written addendum hereto.

OUR AGREEMENT

This Agreement ("Agreement") is made and entered into on the DAY of MONTH, YEAR, between *Terry Stafford*, an independent contractor, hereafter referred to as "Editor," and the author, *Anthony Writer*, hereafter referred to as "Client," for the editing of the manuscript titled **Wonderful Book Title** (approximately **29,500 words**) by The Editor for The Client.

In consideration of the covenants and conditions set forth herein, The Editor and The Client agree as follows:

1. **SERVICES.** For payment as specified below, Editor agrees to provide the following tasks for Client: Select one below.

○ Copy Editing: Correcting errors *(spelling, grammar, punctuation, and consistency mistakes)*—$.04/word **[this job=$nnnn]**

○ Line Editing: Improving language *(reorganizing sentences and paragraphs for clarity, pointing out trouble spots, indicating where something might confuse a reader, generally improving the flow and tone)*—$.045/word **[this job=$nnnn]**

○ Proofreading: Final post-edit read-through just before going to print *(preferably when interior layout is complete)*—$0.02/word **[this job=$nnnn]**

If Client wishes for any further changes to be made, the manuscript is to be returned to Editor, who will incorporate those changes or corrections into the manuscript at the rate of $40 USD per hour (one hour minimum with fractions of an hour rounded up).

1. DELIVERY – Contingent upon the immediate (digital) signing of this contract, prompt payment (as agreed) of the deposit and delivery of the complete draft manuscript, the completed copyedit is to be delivered to Client by Editor on or before **MONTH DAY, YEAR**.

2. PAYMENT – Client agrees to pay Editor **$nnn.00** USD for all services requested above. A **$nnn.00** (50%) deposit is required upon acceptance of this Agreement via electronic signature in order to reserve a spot on my calendar. A digital invoice will be provided for online payment. The remaining **$nnn.00.** balance is due at completion and delivery of the edited manuscript. Initial payment is due upon receipt of the invoice (or as otherwise agreed) with a late fee of $10 per day accumulating beyond that date.

3. METHOD – The preferred payment option is PayPal Business Payments. Credit cards are otherwise not accepted. If Client would like to pay by card, cash, or check, inquire for details BEFORE signing this Agreement.

4. COMPLETION – If Editor has not received any feedback or comments within two weeks of submitting the completed work to The Client (whether the initial draft or subsequent edits), The Editor shall assume the work has been accepted as satisfactorily completed and will conclude the transaction, which will trigger an invoice for the remaining balance.

5. CONFIDENTIALITY – The Editor agrees not to reproduce, give copies, or show to anyone any material provided by The Client except to a subcontractor for editing purposes.

6. LIMITATIONS – No guarantees are made as to the salability or marketability of the edited manuscript. Nor is there a guarantee that the manuscript is 100% error-free, though all efforts will be made to achieve as close to error-free as possible (according to the editing service outlined in this Agreement). Please bear in mind that traditional publishers have three or more editors working on each manuscript, and this Agreement is for one pass by one editor through the document. Customer satisfaction is our #1 priority, so if the Client is dissatisfied with the completed work for any reason, they should contact The Editor immediately.

7. ROYALTIES – Unless a co-writing/co-authorship agreement is made in writing, all royalties and all monies gained by the text shall be the sole property of the Author. Although, The Editor reserves the right to display, make reference to, and link to The Client's completed project as part of the Editor's portfolio.

8. APPLICABLE LAWS – Both parties agree that the language herein shall be interpreted and governed by the laws of the State of California.

9. MISCELLANEOUS – This Agreement may be amended in writing and will only be valid when signed (digitally) by both parties.

10. TERMINATION – Once the project is in progress, either party may

terminate this Agreement in the event of a material change of circumstances with 14-day notice in writing to the other party explaining the circumstances. If the Editor terminates the Agreement, The Client will pay for the work done up to the date of the termination. The Editor will refund any overpayment. If Client terminates the Agreement, The Client will pay The Editor for work completed up to the date of termination, but not be less than 50% of the estimated total cost for the project.

The Client: **The Editor:**

By: _____   By: _____

NAME   *NAME*

Author   Editor

Author Checklist

✓	TASK
	Ideation: Determine what your book will be about, characters, locations, scenes, ending.
	Determine when and where you will write.
	Gather your writing tools.
	Determine launch day or completion day and back date your milestones/due dates.
	Write, Write, Write.
	Perform a self-editing pass of your manuscript.
	Schedule your editor, cover designer, interior layout designer, proofreader, and copywriter.
	Submit manuscript to your editor.
	Order your book cover.
	Order your back-cover copy.
	Incorporate editor change recommendations to your manuscript.
	Submit manuscript to your interior layout designer with requested finish size and style template.
	Provide final page count and paper color to your book cover designer along with ISBN, LCCN.
	Provide final back-cover copy to your book cover designer.
	Submit interior file to proofreader.
	Submit changes to interior layout designer.
	Upload final cover and final interior file to Amazon KDP and/or Ingram Spark (or others).
	Await Amazon (and Ingram Spark) title acceptance email.
	Order proof copies.
	Approve final book for launch.
	Order sales and giveaway copies. Enjoy the ride!

Who is Terry?

Award-winning author, Terry Stafford, came to writing later in life. He uses his fiction to weave tales of music and hope for readers who miss the good ol' days. Having a master's degree in management as well as a background in the U.S. Navy and later with NASA as a senior project manager, Terry saw how his experience could bring order out of creative chaos in his own writing life. He knows creatives often feel like scatter-brained writers and helps them become organized, prolific storytellers. Terry lives in California's beautiful San Joaquin Valley with his wife, Gail. Both talented musicians, you can find them attending bluegrass music festivals or playing with the praise band every Friday night for the Celebrate Recovery ministry at their church.

Other titles by Terry Stafford,
available online wherever books are sold.

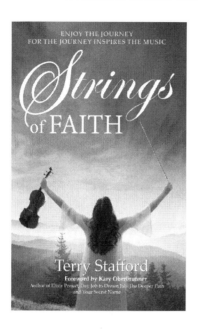

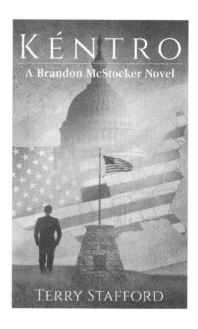

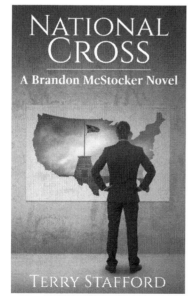

Keep up with Terry's writing and learn about his Project Management for Writers coaching program by visiting his website and subscribing to his newsletter at

https://ItsaWriterfulLife.com

You can also follow Terry on these social media channels:

Facebook [https://www.facebook.com/TerryStaffordAuthor/]

LinkedIn [https://www.linkedin.com/in/terrystafford/]

Instagram [https://www.instagram.com/terrystaffordauthor/]

Pinterest [https://www.pinterest.com/stafford1303/]

QUICK FAVOR

Did you enjoy this book?

First of all, thank you for reading Project Management for Writers! May I ask you a quick favor?

Will you take a moment to leave an honest review for this book on Amazon?

Reviews are the BEST way to help others find and purchase the book.

After that, feel free to share your thoughts with me directly at the address below.

I appreciate you!

Terry@TerryStafford.com

Made in the USA
Columbia, SC
05 May 2021